MOTHER ANGELICA
ON CHRIST AND OUR LADY

Also by Mother Angelica:

Praying with Mother Angelica
Meditations on the Rosary,
the Way of the Cross,
and Other Prayers

Mother Angelica's
Answers, Not Promises

MOTHER ANGELICA
ON CHRIST AND
OUR LADY

EWTN PUBLISHING, INC.
Irondale, Alabama

Mother Angelica on Christ and Our Lady was originally published as five mini-books: *In His Sandals* (1973), *Love Is Not Loved* (1976), *The Divine Personality of Jesus* (1976), *The Fruits of His Love* (1977), and *The Promised Woman* (1977), copyright Our Lady of the Angels Monastery 3222 County Road 548, Hanceville, Alabama 35077, www.olamshrine.com, and printed with the ecclesiastical approval of Joseph G. Vath, D.D., Bishop of Birmingham, Alabama, USA.

Printed in the United States of America. All rights reserved.

Cover and interior design by Perceptions Design Studio.

Cover art: detail from official portrait by John Howard Sanden.

All quotations from Holy Scripture are taken from Jerusalem Bible, © 1966 by Darton Longman and Todd Ltd. and Doubleday and Company Ltd.

EWTN Publishing, Inc.
5817 Old Leeds Road, Irondale, AL 35210

Distributed by Sophia Institute Press, Box 5284, Manchester, NH 03108.

Library of Congress Cataloging-in-Publication Data

Names: M. Angelica (Mary Angelica), Mother, 1923-2016, author.
Title: Mother Angelica on Christ and Our Lady.
Description: Irondale, Alabama : EWTN Publishing, Inc., 2016.
Identifiers: LCCN 2016040910 | ISBN 9781682780121 (hardcover : alk. paper)
Subjects: LCSH: Jesus Christ—Biography.
Classification: LCC BT301.3 .M25 2016 | DDC 232—dc23 LC record available at https://lccn.loc.gov/2016040910

First printing

CONTENTS

The Divine Personality of Jesus

The Fruits of His Love

In His Sandals

Love Is Not Loved

Editor's Note

This volume brings together for the first time *The Divine Personality of Jesus*, *The Fruits of His Love*, *In His Sandals*, *Love Is Not Loved*, and *The Promised Woman*, five "mini-books" written by Mother Angelica and published by Our Lady of the Angels Monastery in the 1970s. Each section of this book corresponds to one of Mother's original mini-books. Taken together, they form a unique and beautiful work of spiritual wisdom and prayerful reverence.

Mother Angelica wrote these words on a pad of paper while in Adoration of the Blessed Sacrament in the chapel of her monastery in Irondale, Alabama. Her order, the Poor Clares of Perpetual Adoration, has been dedicated to the Blessed Sacrament since its founding, and so it is only fitting that Mother's written works were completed in His Presence.

By the mid-1970s, the Nuns of Our Lady of the Angels Monastery were printing as many as twenty-five thousand copies of these mini-books and others per day. This was truly a nascent mass-media operation, one that would lead to the creation of EWTN—the Eternal Word Television Network.

This book is a faithful representation of Mother Angelica's original work, with only the most basic corrections of printing errors, adjustments to formatting, and so on. You can be confident that you are reading an authentic presentation of the wisdom and spirituality of one of the most important figures in the history of Catholicism in America.

MOTHER ANGELICA
ON CHRIST AND
OUR LADY

THE PROMISED WOMAN

EVE: THE FIRST WOMAN

In the beginning, when God created Adam, it was soon apparent that there was something lacking.

The magnificent beauty of the new creation lacked a dimension. Adam must have looked around and tried to find out exactly what was missing.

The whole world was literally his and yet he was not completely satisfied. He needed someone to share the fruits of his work as he tilled the soil and made things grow (Gen. 2:5).

God saw this and said, "It is not good for man to be alone. I will make him a helpmate." So He fashioned all the wild beasts and the birds and brought them to Adam to name them (Gen. 2:18).

It is strange that in this second account God chose animals to help Adam in his work and be a comfort to him.

But Adam was filled with one of God's beautiful perfections — Goodness. He wanted to share his joy and happiness with someone — someone like himself.

But no helpmate *suitable* for Adam was found, and so, the account goes on, God cast Adam into a deep sleep and from his rib formed Eve (Gen. 2:21).

God blessed them, saying to them, "Be fruitful, multiply, fill the earth and conquer it. Be masters of the fish of the sea, the birds of heaven, and all living animals of the earth" (Gen. 1:28).

Adam and Eve were created in the image of God. They were above all creation because they were intelligent human beings. They shared something with all created things — mineral life, vegetable life, animal life, and angelic life; the two of them were truly the culmination of all God's creation.

He told them to be fruitful, to be masters of all animal life, and to conquer the world.

The world, then, was something to conquer, and He gave them many gifts by which to do it.

The soil was easy to till — everything Adam did was successful — he was never weary, dull-witted, or at a loss for what to do.

His mental faculties were in perfect control; his will was centered on God, his understanding saw God in all creation, his memory was filled with God's goodness to him, and his imagination was at peace in regard to the past and filled with hope in regard to the future.

And so it was with Eve. Neither one had to fight those dispositions that make life intolerable at times.

They loved each other and were in perfect control of every situation.

There were no frustrations, no tensions, no worries. They had a perfect relationship between themselves and with God.

Everything came easy, as their physical and mental powers were at their best.

Scripture does not say how long they lived before the test came, but their life together in God's new creation was no doubt as perfect as it could be this side of heaven.

With so many gifts and talents, it was only fair and necessary that they be given the opportunity to choose between God and themselves.

Without a test, their freewill would not have been free. The Garden of Paradise was so beautiful that their will was held captive by the joy and happiness of that place.

Perhaps this was the beginning of their fall.

Perhaps they became so enamored with their gifts and talents that they began to attribute them to themselves.

Perhaps they lost sight of the fact that everything they had had come from God and that He alone was supreme over all.

Perhaps their gratitude began to wane as their self-infatuation became greater.

Whatever the cause, one thing is sure: the serpent instilled the seed of pride into Eve's mind and it overpowered her. She decided she would be like God—not out of love but in an effort to be superior—equal to God.

She convinced Adam that he, too, should stand alone—independent of God. After all, he was superior to everything in the world, lord of the animal kingdom, and his intelligence was like the angels.

Surely, the fruit of their labor was *their* fruit, the beauty of the garden was the result of *their* planning and *their* efforts.

Surely, they could decide and rule by themselves—with no help from anyone.

They were warned not to partake of the forbidden fruit —the tree of knowledge between good and evil; they were to enjoy the gifts they had received and be grateful children of a loving Father.

God did not intend that they should experience their limitations, their weakness, and their incapabilities.

His Love, Providence, and Wisdom would care for them as only a loving God can—they were to trust and be grateful.

But the father of lies, who fell because he attributed all his gifts to himself, and in his pride refused to serve, tempted Eve to break away from God's dominion and create one of her own—a place where she and Adam would decide what was good and what was evil.

They were told by God to multiply, be masters, and conquer the world.

But when they began to take their eyes away from God and concentrate them on themselves, the world conquered them, and the world became their master.

Suddenly, their pride stripped them naked: all the gifts that made life easy and kept their passions under control were gone.

They saw themselves as they really were—nothing—nothing but finite, weak, human beings—human beings, slow of comprehension, victims of their own passions, and very much aware of themselves.

The truth of what they were, without God's gifts must have been a shattering experience.

They saw their nothingness and were ashamed.

They covered themselves and hid because they suddenly realized the great difference between themselves and God.

Fear was born. It replaced the childlike simplicity they possessed when they were grateful children of a loving Father.

They had been told that if they ate this fruit they would die. They expected a physical death then and there: but pride is first a spiritual death and it brought with it all the consequences of that kind of death—evil tendencies, unruly passions, bitterness, regrets, and darkness.

God had to tell them the consequences of their decision.

First, He addressed the serpent—the master of pride—and told him that from henceforth he would crawl on his belly and eat dust.

Every human being would look down upon this once angel of light and regard him as dust—an enemy to be trampled on and avoided—avoided by everyone except those who, like himself, decided that dust was what they wanted to be.

His pride caused his fall from heaven; his pride incited Eve to imitation—but now, all men would see him as he is—a spirit of darkness. The war that ended in heaven began on earth.

And then the Mercy of God came through as Beautiful as it is Infinite. He told the father of lies that He would set another Woman against him and her seed would crush his head.

A new Adam and a new Eve would come and these two would not disappoint Him. They would be mortal enemies of the serpent and crush his head — his pride — with their holiness and humility.

This Messianic prophecy declared war between the two kingdoms. Some of Eve's descendants would choose one side and some the other. But there would be two people who would crush the tempter's pride.

The tempter rejoiced that he had seemingly spoiled God's plan through a weak woman. God would use a weak Woman to crush his head.

Through Eve and her seed pride came into the world and with it every other evil. Through another Woman and her seed God would redeem the world. He would bless it with greater opportunities — so great that those who corresponded would be called "sons of God."

These children would rejoice that their Creator was Father, Master, and Lord over them.

Through the Woman, the Father would give the world His Son, for only His Son could redeem the world.

To Eve the Father gave a distressing message. Her pain during child-bearing would be multiplied; she would yearn for her husband but he would be more master than lover. She, who refused to be under God's dominion, would be under man's dominion.

To Adam He addressed words of disappointment and rebuke. Adam had chosen to listen to Eve rather than to God. He made a choice that stripped him of strength and dignity.

From now on, what had been easy would be difficult.

The rich soil that had yielded such an abundance of fruit would harden itself against him and yield fruit with difficulty.

The joy of working was turned into the sweat of hard labor—labor that would cause a fatigue he had never known before.

Finally, after long years of hardship and toil, he would return to the dust from which he came.

It was not a curse: it was a choice—Adam's and Eve's. But God, in His Infinite Mercy, would not leave them naked.

Though their pride stripped them of preternatural gifts, He would clothe them with natural gifts—gifts that would be an aid in this valley of tears.

As children were born to them, they inherited their tendencies, passions, labor, and death.

But throughout the centuries one ray of light shone in the darkness—a Woman would come and her seed would give back more than was lost.

MARY: THE PROMISED WOMAN

As the centuries passed and mankind lived in more darkness and became more depraved, God would send His prophets to encourage and enlighten His creatures.

Though His creatures chose to rule themselves, He would not abandon them.

He would send them glimpses of what was to come through His Prophets. He would intervene in their history to show His Power. He would forgive their many transgressions to manifest His Mercy.

Through Noah, the Father showed His Mercy by preserving the human race, because of the holiness of one man.

Through Abraham, He gave an example of Faith and Hope —Faith in an invisible God, and Hope in His promises. He tested that Faith when He asked Abraham to sacrifice His only son, to prefigure the sacrifice He Himself would make, by giving His Son to redeem the world.

Through Abraham He began to form a small nation of people through whom He would manifest His love and Mercy by sending His Son.

Abraham was to prefigure the Father's Love. He was willing to sacrifice his son in obedience to God's command. But Abraham's son was spared — God's Son was condemned.

Through Jacob, God brought forth the twelve tribes of Israel. From one of these tribes would come His Son and the Woman.

He showed Jacob a ladder in a dream, with angels going up and coming down. His Son would be the ladder between heaven and earth, uniting two worlds separated by a great gulf.

Through Joseph, God prefigured His Son, Jesus. Jesus, like Joseph, would be sold for a few pieces of silver, and the Father would use man's jealousy to redeem His people.

Through Moses He showed the mystery of all mysteries.

The burning bush prefigured the God-man who was to come. A bush on fire yet ever green symbolized the union of Divinity with humanity.

It also prefigured the future role of the Woman who was to come — a Woman who was on fire with love for God and became a Mother, yet always remained a Virgin.

Again, He chose one man — Moses — to deliver His people from bondage. He gave him laws through which they would find God.

Time and time again they defied His laws, and time and time again He used their depravity to show His Mercy and form a people through which His Son would come.

His Presence hovered over them as a cloud during the day and as fire during the night.

But despite His care they often complained against God and Moses. As with Adam and Eve, so these people rebelled against God's authority. They were bitten by fiery serpents and many died.

Then Moses interceded for his people, and God used this incident to prefigure His Son on the Cross and its healing power.

He commanded Moses to make a fiery serpent and put it on a standard and all who looked upon it would be healed. In the same way, those who would look upon His Son on the Cross and repent, would be healed of their sins.

As time went on, He prefigured and foretold ...

- His Son's priesthood and immolation, in Leviticus,
- His Son's Presence in the midst of His people, in Numbers,
- His Son's law of the Gospels, in Deuteronomy,
- His Son's conducting His creatures to the Promised Land, in Joshua,
- the power of penance and repentance, in Judges,
- His Son's patience in adversity, and future Resurrection, in Job,
- the power of prayer and humility, in the life of David,
- and His Son's Birth, Life, and Death, in Isaias and Jeremias.

Throughout these centuries He also prefigured and foretold the mission and the coming of the Woman — the Woman He promised to Adam and Eve — the one who would crush the serpent's head.

- Deborah, Judith, and Esther prefigured the Woman whose holiness God would use to deliver His people from the enemy.
- Through Isaias He promised a Virgin who would conceive and bring forth a Son whose name would be

Emanuel—a son who would "bear His Kingdom on His shoulders, and He would be called Wonder-Counselor, Mighty-God, Eternal-Father, and Prince of Peace." (Is. 7:14; 9:6)

❧ Through Jeremias He announces that the Woman will bear in her womb a man who is God and man. (Jer. 31:21-22)

Ezekiel saw the Woman in the figure of a closed gate which was open only for God and through which no other man could enter (Ezek. 44:2).

In the Canticle of Canticles, her grace and beauty are so great that they capture the Heart of God, and He is enraptured with the love of her virginal heart.

Though she slept, her heart was always awake, and, unlike Eve whose yearning met only with man's authority, the Woman finds Love. "I am my Beloved's and His desire is for me" (Cant. 7:11).

Unlike Eve, whose pride forced Adam to wield the hand of authority, the Woman breaks through the clouds of sin like the soft rays of the sun—penetrating and coloring everything they touch, but never casting a shadow over the sun.

As Eve desired to be in a position of authority, the Woman was satisfied to be His Handmaid.

As Eve desired to experience good and evil, the Woman was desirous of casting her eyes upon Goodness alone.

As Eve desired to be in a position of authority, the Woman was His humble servant.

As Eve glorified herself, the Woman exulted in the Lord.

As Eve desired to be in the first place, the Woman found joy in the last place.

As Eve took the credit for her gifts, the Woman magnified the Lord that His Power had done great things in her.

And so it was that as Eve's pride made her the mother of fallen mankind, the Woman's humility made her the Mother of God.

THE GOOD NEWS

The seventy weeks prophesied by Daniel were drawing to a close and another prophet was soon to appear.

"The voice crying in the wilderness: make straight his paths. Every valley must be filled and every mountain laid low" was soon to be heard.

The time for the lowly to be exalted and the proud to be humbled had come.

An Angel of the Lord, Gabriel, who had spoken to Daniel, speaks to the priest, Zechariah, as he offers incense in the Temple.

Zechariah, like Daniel, was a man of desires, but age and disappointment had weakened those desires, and though he had prayed for a son, now he no longer prayed—it was too late.

The Angel told Zechariah that his wife, Elizabeth, would bear a son and that his name would be John.

Poor Zechariah had been disappointed too many times to believe even an angel and he doubted the Angel's word.

How little human nature has changed!

How often, like Zechariah, have we asked and asked, and then when the time comes for God to say yes, He finds only incredulity.

But God's Will is not dependent upon man's will, and Gabriel told Zechariah that the son who was soon to be his would be great before the Lord.

He would be filled with the Holy Spirit from his mother's womb. He would turn the hearts of fathers towards their children and the disobedient back to wisdom and the virtuous way.

He would prepare the way of the Lord (Lk. 1:13-17).

It would seem that this announcement would have filled the old man with ecstatic joy, but his faith had grown weak and he merely answered, "How can I be sure of this? I am an old man and my wife is getting on in years."

The answer he received was not one of understanding and compassion. If joyous news would not shake the shackles of doubt loose, then suffering would, as it did in the past when God's People became stiff-necked and unbelieving.

"I am Gabriel who stand in God's Presence," the Angel told Zechariah. "I have been sent to speak to you and bring you this good news. Listen, since you have not believed my words, which will come true at their appropriate time, you will be silenced and have no power of speech until this has happened" (Lk. 1:19-20).

Zechariah received the sign he wanted and the only sign that in his frame of mind he would have understood. He lost his speech — struck dumb — but was finally happy that his long prayer was soon to be answered.

Did the angel of darkness, the serpent, sense that the time the Prophets foretold had come? Surely, with his great intelligence and memory, he never lost sight of and never ceased hearing the curses heaped upon him in the Garden of Eden.

God told him a woman would conceive and He would put enmity between her seed and his seed, and she would crush his head.

He must have stalked the earth looking for this Virgin, prophesied by Isaiah, who would conceive and bear a son.

He must have mistaken many women throughout the centuries, only to be disappointed when these holy maidens became betrothed.

He must have wondered what it all meant. Was the Virgin who was to conceive not to be married, or if she were married why call her a virgin?

What did it mean? Where was she? When would she come?

Would she be so holy that everyone would recognize her as someone very unusual? Yes, if he were God, He would do it that way.

He would make her birth a day never to be forgotten—something unusual would be in order.

As a child she would certainly be set apart and kept alone in order to prepare her for the great occasion.

Yes, she would have to be famous and popular, and then when *she* conceived, all men would wait with great expectation for God's Son.

The heavens would thunder, the voice of the Father would proclaim His Birth and all men would tremble.

And so the angel of darkness looked for all the signs of pride—pride, the only thing he knew—and he looked and looked but never seemed to find the woman or her Son.

The great deceiver was about to be deceived.

In Elizabeth's sixth month the Angel Gabriel appeared to a young virgin betrothed to a man named Joseph. Her name was Mary—a very common name among the Jewish people.

Scripture does not say she was disturbed at seeing the Angel—only at his words. Had she seen him before? And why would his words disturb her?

It was the dream of every Jewish woman to be the mother of the Messiah.

Why was she troubled when the Angel said, "Rejoice, so highly favored! The Lord is with you"? (Lk. 1:28).

She was deeply disturbed at these words. Her great humility made her wonder what these words meant.

She was told not to be afraid because she had won the favor of God. And then came the message prophets and kings had waited to hear and did not hear.

"Listen," he said, "you are to conceive and bear a son, and you must name him Jesus. He will be great and will be called 'Son of the Most High.'"

Mary replied, "But how can this come about, since I am a virgin?" (Lk. 1:34).

All Jewish children were well instructed in the ways of life. Why would one betrothed ask such a question?

She had just been told she was to be the Mother of the Messiah.

And yet, she asked how this could be. She was a virgin and intended to remain so.

How was her desire to give herself totally to God and yet to become the Mother of the Messiah compatible?

It was a question in her mind as it has been a question in the minds of generations to follow.

How would this be done?

"The Holy Spirit will come upon you," the Angel answered, "and the power of the Most High will cover you with its shadow. And so, the Child will be holy and will be called Son of God."

The answer to her question was a mystery and so the Angel continued, "Know this too, your kinswoman, Elizabeth, has, in her old age, herself conceived a son, and she whom people called barren is now in her sixth month, *for nothing is impossible to God.*"

Unlike Zechariah who doubted it could be done, Mary merely asked how it would be done.

Now she knew she would bear a Son through the Holy Spirit and remain a virgin.

But one thing was necessary before this great mystery would be enacted: Her Will must be firmly rooted in God's Will.

As man had fallen through the selfish choice of a woman who tempted a man to pride, so the Woman must freely choose God and bring forth a Man of Humility.

This Man and Woman would say together, "Holocaust and sin offering you would not, but a body you have fitted me—behold, I come to do Your Will" (Heb. 10:5-7).

As all of Heaven wanted to see what choice this Woman would make, she folded her hands across her breast, cast her eyes down, and said, "I am the Handmaid of the Lord; let what you have said be done to me" (Lk. 1:38).

And then the same Power that said to nothingness, "Be made," enveloped the Woman like a shadow—elevated her to a state of union with God unheard of before and un-thought-of since.

The beginning of the new Kingdom had come. As the "No" of one woman brought misery and darkness upon the world, so the "yes" of another Woman brought grace and peace to mankind.

If Isaiah and Jeremiah found comfort in the realization that they were known by God before creation and in their mothers' wombs, how much more was this Woman known and loved by God from all Eternity?

As the Father saw Eve disappoint Him, He saw Mary prefer Him; she was truly His obedient daughter.

As our union with God must be with all Three Persons, so Mary's union progressed from Daughter of the Father, to Spouse of the Holy Spirit, to Mother of the Son.

The new Eve renewed what the old Eve had lost—union with the Trinity.

As we all inherited misery from Eve, we can all partake of the privileges of the Woman.

We, too, are daughters of the Father. We, too, can be spouses of the Spirit. We, too, can be mothers of the Son, for Her Son was one day to say that he who did the Will of His Father was His brother, mother, and sister:

Brother as sharing the same Father—Mother as sharing the same nature—Sister as sharing the same Spirit.

All this because, like the Woman, our wills are firmly rooted in His.

She did what God desired Eve to do—prefer Him to herself that we in turn may do the same.

And so, the Woman and her Seed had come and the Tempter knew it not.

CONCERN

It would be natural, after being told by an Angel of God's favor, being overshadowed by the Holy Spirit, and conceiving the Son of God, that the Woman would have remained in her home, alone and undisturbed.

Certainly this would be a time to ponder the mystery within her and converse with the Father as to her role in the Mystery of Redemption.

But Scripture says that Mary made haste and went to visit her cousin Elizabeth.

Her concern for her aged cousin carrying a child drove her to leave her home and her espoused husband to help Elizabeth in her time of need.

As she traveled the five miles to the hill country of Judah she must have thought about her Son.

It must have been a frightening and awesome meditation to think of carrying Omnipotence in such a tiny chamber.

In her modesty she would have kept her secret, but God had other plans. As soon as Elizabeth heard Mary's greeting, she was filled with the Holy Spirit and with a loud voice proclaimed that Mary was the Woman.

"Of all women you are the most blessed," she said, "and blessed is the fruit of your womb" (Lk. 1:42).

Like all fathers, God could not keep the wonderful secret too long. He had to tell someone, and that someone was Elizabeth carrying the child who was to be His Son's forerunner.

For such a mission, this child of Elizabeth, like Jeremiah, must be sanctified in his mother's womb.

The Presence of the Father's Son in Mary sanctified the child in Elizabeth.

Elizabeth was so filled with the Holy Spirit that she cried out, "Why should I be so honored with a visit from the mother of my Lord? For the moment your greeting reached my ears, the child in my womb leapt for joy."

It is common for a child in the womb to move, and Elizabeth had felt movement before. It was a sign of life. But this movement was different; it was as if her child recognized His Creator and knelt in adoration—it was a sign of supernatural life.

Elizabeth's soul filled with joy; she looked at Mary and said, "Blessed art thou among women and blessed is the fruit of thy womb" (Lk. 1:42).

Unlike Eve who took praise to herself, Mary lifted her soul to God as a humble servant of the Most High. Her knowledge of Scripture was superb and she quoted His words. She prayed the words of Scripture as given in Isaiah, Samuel, Habacuc, Genesis, Psalms, Ezekiel, and Job, and her voice rang out with a hymn of praise (Lk. 1:46-55):

My soul proclaims the Greatness of the Lord, and my spirit exults in God my Savior.

Her whole being found its joy in God and in God alone. He was great in her—she would exult in His perfections as manifested in her soul,

Because He has looked upon His lowly handmaid.

She would always be a handmaid, content that He was Master and Lord. Eve desired to be her own master but the Promised Woman would desire only the truth. The truth is, that He alone is Holy and He alone is Lord.

Truly, He would look with pleasure upon her adherence to the truth that He alone is Supreme, and she could say,

Yes, from this day forward all generations shall call me blessed for the Almighty has done great things in me. Holy is His Name.

Her only thought is of God. She acknowledges His gifts but never attributes them to any personal merit. It is His Goodness and His Love and His Holiness that have accomplished these great things. He drew her out of nothingness because

His Mercy reaches from age to age for those who fear Him.

The fear of the Lord filled her pure heart. It was the fear that comes from love—a filial relationship with God as Father.

She was His daughter, formed by His hands in her mother's womb, with a soul that came from the breath of God. Yes,

He has shown the power of His arm; He has routed the proud of heart.

The preparing of her pure soul by the Holy Spirit, as a fit dwelling place for the Son's humanity, was a greater act of

Omnipotence than the creation of the whole universe. The proud would flee from her humility because

He has pulled down princes from their thrones and exalted the lowly.

The Angel of Darkness and all his adherents fell from heaven like lightning. The father of lies attributed his beauty and perfections to himself; Eve attributed her gifts to herself—and both fell from their thrones because God exalts the lowly.

The lowly are not those who *feel* inferior, for that too is a lie—but those who acknowledge the source of their talents, gifts, life, and grace—God, the Giver of all good things.

For the hungry He has filled with good things; the rich He has sent away empty.

Mary hungered only for God. His Will, difficult though it might be, would be her food, and He would fill her with every grace.

But those who are proud, rich in themselves, possessing their own soul for their own pleasure, *those* He would send away empty.

The Woman had come from the chosen people; she knew their needs and the needs of the world, and she rejoiced that,

He has come to the help of Israel, His servant, mindful of His Mercy — according to the promise He made to our ancestors — of His Mercy to Abraham and to his descendants forever.

After three months Mary returned to Nazareth. She had been proclaimed the most blessed among women, and she carried in her womb, God's Son.

She left Judah as quietly and unnoticed as she had arrived, and the Deceiver knew her not.

TRUST

The joy of the visit to Elizabeth soon gave way to anguish of spirit. Only one who has been under suspicion would understand the feelings of her pure heart when she arrived home and Joseph began to cast questioning glances.

It is not recorded in Scripture that she uttered one word in her defense. She had learned to trust every detail of her life to God.

She carried His Son; He would uphold her honor.

But day after day it became more obvious to Joseph that she was with child.

He loved her too much and understood her too well to question her integrity, but he knew that the Child she carried was not his.

They were espoused, but Scripture says he did not know her. Had he also taken a vow of virginity? They were espoused at least six months, and yet he was puzzled.

He saw Mary, the joy of his heart, day after day, and his heart ached. He could not sleep or work, and the more attention she gave him at meals or in the shop, the more anguish filled his heart.

And what of Mary? Her loving heart must have been broken to see one so loving in such distress. Should she tell him what really happened? Would he believe such a mystery? Was it her place to explain? How many questions must have filled her mind!

No one knew how the Messiah would come, and although His coming was prophesied and foretold centuries ago, the reality was so different.

No, she would pray and wait for God's time. What profound faith it must have taken! What deep hope she needed to carry on her duties in silence and love!

To see Joseph suffer so much must have wrenched her heart many times. It is always difficult to see those we love suffer, and we would go to any length to help alleviate their pain.

And yet, Mary—that valiant woman—would not explain, even though her silence meant more anguish for Joseph.

The one thing they had in common was their sorrow. Each wanted to speak to the other—one to ask "Why?"—the other to answer "How," but neither one spoke a word of what weighed heavy on his heart.

They must have spoken of other things—his work and her chores, God and the Temple, the beauty of His nature, and the needs of His people, but they never spoke of the issue behind all issues.

By whom was this Woman with child?

She was too lovely, kind, and holy to be doubted, but one thing Joseph knew—he was not the father.

He was a just man who loved God above all things and it never crossed his mind that his espoused wife might be the Promised Woman.

He knew she was special and this is what made it so difficult to do what he knew he must.

He could not bring himself to expose her to public ridicule but neither could he pretend the child was his, and so he decided to divorce her privately.

Mary must have sensed his dilemma and prayed to the Father for a solution that would set Joseph's heart at rest.

The time of suffering and purification was over, and an Angel of the Lord appeared to Joseph in his sleep and said, "Joseph, son of David, do not be afraid to take Mary home as your wife, because she has conceived what is in her by the Holy Spirit."

"She will give birth to a son and you must name Him Jesus, because He is the One who is to save His people from their sins" (Mt. 1:20-21).

What overwhelming joy and consternation must have filled his heart: joy, that at last he understood; and consternation, when he realized that he had almost left her.

It is hard to imagine the moment when his glance met hers and she understood that he knew.

He must have wept with joy and knelt in prayer before the living Ark of the Covenant — the Holy Temple in which dwelt, in a physical manner, the Son of God.

And now, three people knew, but the Deceiver knew it not.

OBEDIENCE

It is hard to imagine the loving atmosphere in the house of Nazareth as Mary's time approached.

Mary must have prepared all the little things a future mother prepares. And Joseph must have made a crib that rivaled all cribs.

They studied the Scriptures with great fervor, looking for glimpses of what this Child would be. There must have been moments of joy and fear as they read that He would be filled with the Holy Spirit but also be a Man of Sorrows.

They would try to forget the pain this Child would endure and think only of His coming birth and the joy of that moment.

They spoke of nothing else and waited with great expectation. And then, one day, when Joseph went to the market place, he saw a decree from Caesar Augustus asking for a census of the Empire.

His heart sank as he realized what it meant. He and Mary must go to the town of David, called Bethlehem, and register, for they were both from the house of David.

How would he tell Mary? How would she ever make the journey? Perhaps if they started early and took the journey in slow stages she would be able to make it. These, and many more questions, must have raced through his mind as he went home to tell Mary the news.

Mary assured him that all would be well. Her faith in the Father's Providence and Love knew no bounds, and they would manage.

Did she think of the Prophet Micheas when he said, "And you, Bethlehem, in the land of Judah, you are by no means least among the leaders of Judah, for out of you will come a Leader who will shepherd my people Israel" (Mic. 5:2).

If this passage passed through their minds at all, it was little consolation. The thought of Mary giving birth in an unknown city, among strangers, must have been a possibility Joseph erased from his mind. No, they would go and hurry back so that he could care for her and the Child.

And so they began the journey from Nazareth to Bethlehem. It must have been an arduous one, not so much because of the distance as the circumstances and pressures under which they traveled.

The roads were crowded with men, women, children, camels, and caravans. The young couple must have been jostled back and forth from the surge of the crowds, all going to various towns to register—all of them angered and ill-tempered at the decree of a pagan Emperor who demanded that God's chosen people be registered like herds of cattle.

Through it all Joseph kept looking at Mary to see if he could be of any assistance, only to be comforted by her reassuring smile that all was well.

Joseph had great confidence that the Father would provide a worthy dwelling place for this Woman of all women. There would be relatives in Bethlehem who, like him, had gone to register and they would all be together.

They were poor but he would get the best room in one of the inns for his wife to rest until he could register.

But when they arrived, he found conditions in Bethlehem were worse than he had anticipated. The crowds were dense, the soldiers short-tempered, and the inns filled.

His heart sank. What was he to do? He went from inn to inn only to be turned away. He couldn't believe it. Was there no place? How could this be? His wife was with Child — God's own Son — surely the Provident God would provide some suitable shelter? But there was no place in the inns — not one small place.

He went back to Mary and she gave him that understanding smile that always quieted his doubts when things went wrong.

He gently helped Mary on to the donkey and turned towards the city gate. On the way he noticed a shelter — a cave where shepherds and innkeepers kept animals in bad weather.

His heart gave a sigh of relief, but his mind rejected such a place for such a delicate woman.

Mary nodded her head to assure him it was alright. She didn't mind. She understood — it seemed she always understood. Perhaps her love was so great that somehow everything turned to good when she was around.

Joseph led Mary into the cave, took off his cloak and used it as a broom, and then set fresh straw in the corner for Mary to rest on.

He would build a fire near the cave entrance and lie there to protect her from harm or intrusion.

LOVE

Tradition has set the date for Christ's birth as December 25th. During the silence of that blessed night the cave lit up with a heavenly brilliance.

All of Heaven came to that precious cave. It was the Night of nights! The Expected of the nations was about to be born.

Angels arrayed themselves in choirs, and the "silence was, as it were, for a half-hour," and suddenly Mary became transfigured and a male Child came forth from the closed doors of her womb, like the Risen Christ was to issue from the sealed entrance of His Tomb (Rev. 8:1).

The Gate that was never opened remained closed forever as God's Son left the chamber of His temple to redeem His people.

The Hosannas rang through the cave as the Eternal Word-made-Flesh gazed at the beautiful face of His Mother for the first time.

Who can imagine the joy of the Father and the Holy Spirit as they beheld God Incarnate!

The awesomeness of the moment was so electrifying that Joseph woke up to look upon the most beautiful scene in the world — Heaven on Earth.

All the hardships and heartaches seemed to fall away as his heart was filled with ecstatic joy.

Mary motioned for him to come, and he knelt in adoration as she held the Child out to him.

No words would ever express their mutual feelings at that moment. They must have wondered why they were so alone at the moment that prophets and kings longed to see.

Joseph went out of the cave hoping to share the Good News, but it was cold, dark, and lonely. The sound of the night wind seemed to cry out, "There is no room in the inn of these people's hearts."

Generations had prayed, waited, and finally lost heart, and the darkness of the night echoed their dirge.

But the Father was not to permit His Son's birth to go un-announced. An Angel appeared to shepherds on the hillside and said, "Do not be afraid. Listen, I bring you news of great joy — a joy to be shared by the whole people."

"Today in the town of David a Saviour has been born to you; He is Christ the Lord."

It must be proclaimed right from Heaven that the Promised One was here. He, in whose palm all creation rests, had come as a Child to take away our shame.

The Angel continued, "And here is a sign for you: you will find a Baby wrapped in swaddling clothes and lying in a manger" (Lk. 2:10-13).

The Child wanted us to know from the beginning that He came to give and wanted nothing of this world's goods. He was satisfied with the least, that we might not desire the most.

The humble Infant lying in a manger was a sign of the Godhead for the shepherds.

It was then, as it is now, a sign that only the lowly of heart can see and understand.

It is no wonder that the Deceiver saw Him not.

Visitors

The Holy Family had three types of visitors after the birth of the Child Jesus.

Each seemed to represent a segment of humanity that would influence the child's life in the future.

We will look at them in the order of their visitation.

The Shepherds

After the Angel announced Christ's birth, "a great throng of Angels appeared, praising God, and singing":

> Glory to God in the highest Heaven, and peace to men who enjoy His favor. (Lk. 2:13-14)

These shepherds were simple men, accustomed to poverty and want. They would not be scandalized to see God's Son in a manger.

They were men of deep faith—the kind of faith that had grown strong by communing with God during the lonely hours of grazing sheep.

Their intellects were not cluttered with debates and speculations about the Messiah and His mission.

He had only to announce to them the Good News and they believed.

To them, faith was not so much an act of the intellect as an act of the heart. As they would not be scandalized by the poverty of the crib, neither would they be scandalized by the ignominy of the Cross when that time came.

Yes, it was to such as these—the poor in spirit—that the Good News must be announced.

The Rabbi

Scripture says that "When the eighth day came and the Child was to be circumcised, they gave Him the name of Jesus, the name the Angel had given Him before His conception" (Lk. 2:21).

The Child was merely eight days old when He shed His Precious Blood for our redemption.

The sinless One followed a law made for sinners.

The Rabbi must have received many graces for performing this rite, but there is no record of him knowing who the Child was or of having the Good News announced to him.

Why was it that Angels appeared to shepherds and a star to pagan Wise Men but not a word to the Rabbi?

Was it because he should have known by the Scriptures?

Did the Father seek to protect His Son from being known too soon and thereby ruining His mission?

Perhaps the man might have spread the News and Herod would have pursued the Child before He could be presented in the Temple.

And then, perhaps the man who had studied the Law and the Prophets so long had preconceived ideas of what the Messiah would be like, and an Infant in such poverty would not measure up to his expectations.

Whatever the reasons for not revealing His Son, the Father did bring the Old Law face to face with the New Law for the first time. But despite the Rabbi's knowledge and holiness, the crib proved a stumbling block then, as it does now, to the Chosen People.

The Magi

The Shepherds had come to represent the poor, the Rabbi had come to represent the Law, and now the Magi came to represent the Gentiles.

The Infant had come to preach the Good News to the poor, to follow the Law, and to bring salvation to the pagans.

Somehow, three Kings, who perhaps studied the Law and the Prophets of the Chosen People, realized that the time had come for His birth.

Their joy at the realization and their desire to see Him must have been pleasing to the Father. In His foreknowledge, He saw their desires and inspired His Prophets to say:

"Camels in throngs will cover you and dromedaries of Madian and Epha: everyone in Saba will come, bringing gold and incense and singing the praise of God" (Is. 60:6).

The Psalmist wrote: "The Kings of Sheba and Seba will offer gifts; all kings will do Him homage" (Ps. 72:10-11).

And so it was that "after Jesus was born, some Wise Men came to Jerusalem from the East."

"Where is the Infant King of the Jews?" they asked. We saw His star as it rose and have come to do Him homage" (Mt. 2:1-2).

They must have gone to every Rabbi and Teacher and approached passers-by, because Herod soon received the news of foreign Kings looking for the new King.

"New King," Herod thought, "there is no king but me." And so he called the chief priests and scribes and inquired where the Christ was to be born.

"At Bethlehem in Judea," they told him, and immediately jealousy took possession of him, as it did another king — Saul — centuries before.

"He summoned the Wise Men to a private audience and asked them the exact date on which the star appeared, and sent them on to Bethlehem."

"Go, and find out all about the Child," he said, "and when you have found Him, let me know, so that I, too, may go and do Him homage" (Mt. 2:7-8).

What a perfect example of the hypocrisy the new King was one day to condemn. Herod was an evil man who used innocent men as tools to procure evil ends. He was a man who deceived even himself because he thought he was master in his kingdom, but instead, another kingdom was master of him.

However, the Magi did follow Herod's advice and set out for Bethlehem. "And there in front of them was the star they had seen rising; it went forward and halted over the place where the Child was" (Mt. 2:9).

The Magi had followed the miraculous star for a long time. Why did it disappear as soon as they reached Jerusalem?

The missing star forced the Wise Men to seek direction from citizens, high priests, and kings. Was this God's way of announcing the birth of His Son to the upper classes?

Would they have believed Angels from Heaven or a star in the sky? It is strange that the scribes who advised Herod of the time and place of the Messiah's birth, never pursued the matter further.

Perhaps their fear of Herod, who would stand no rival, blotted from their memory any desire to investigate the rumors.

Whatever the reason for their indifference, they could not complain that they were not told.

Truly, this is a mystery and a lesson. It is possible to become so complacent in our beliefs, so positive of the accuracy of our interpretation of His words, and so satisfied with our prayers, that we miss the essence of the message and ignore the Divine Messenger completely.

If "He came unto His own and His own received Him not," then He would go out into the highways and byways and bring in those who were lowly, full of faith, eager and ready to receive His message and His signs in the manner He gave them (Jn. 1:11).

And so the Magi found the house into which the Holy Family had moved, and there they "saw the Child and His Mother Mary, and falling to their knees they did Him homage."

"Then, opening their treasures, they offered Him gifts of gold, and frankincense, and myrrh" (Mt. 2:11).

Joseph and Mary must have been taken aback by these distinguished visitors bearing such precious gifts.

They, no doubt, remained in Bethlehem until the forty days of purification were accomplished. They would offer Jesus to the Father in the great Temple in Jerusalem, for it was truly God's House on earth.

We do not know how long the Magi stayed, but their gifts were symbolic of the Child's Kingship and suffering. Gold, the most precious of all metals, symbolized His great love for His creatures. Frankincense was the symbol of His Divinity, and the Myrrh was to symbolize His future suffering and death.

These are the gifts they gave, but who is to recount the gifts they received from the Infant?

God is never outdone in generosity. They believed a great truth on the basis of little evidence—a Star. How many men since have traveled far and given as much on so small a revelation?

It is written that to whom much is given, much is required, but these men were given little, produced much, and received an abundance.

Would that we descendants of these Gentile believers had as much faith and produced as much fruit.

It is not recorded how long these men stayed for they were warned in a dream to return home by another way. The wheels of jealousy and hatred for the Child had begun to turn in Jerusalem (Mt. 2:12).

What did Mary and Joseph do with the precious gifts they received from the Wise Men? The only solution one can arrive at is that they gave them to the poor. If they kept even the smallest part of the treasure, surely they would have offered it to God at the Presentation in the Temple.

But shortly they were to travel to Jerusalem to fulfill the law of offering the first-born male to the Lord, and they made the offering of the poor: "a pair of turtledoves or two young pigeons" (Lk. 2:24).

Visitors

O, the marvel of the Wisdom of God! A young couple receive the poor, the Gentiles, and the Church in their humble home, in which dwells the Son of God. He is hidden from the wise and prudent—giving much but receiving little in return, and disguised under the Flesh of His Humanity.

And the Deceiver knew Him not.

OFFERING TO GOD

"And when the day came for them to be purified, as laid down by the Law of Moses, they took Him up to Jerusalem to present Him to the Lord" (Lk. 2:22).

The Woman's portion since she received the Good News was one of mixed joy and sorrow.

The Conception and Visitation to Elizabeth were followed by Joseph's anguish.

The hardships of traveling to Bethlehem were followed by the Nativity.

Her ecstatic joy on that occasion was tempered by the first shedding of His Precious Blood at the Circumcision.

A short time later, her soul again rejoiced that foreign kings recognized her Son's dignity and paid Him homage — only to have a sword pierce her heart as she presented her Son in the Temple.

In the valley of tears created by Eve, Mary would show us how to travel its mountain peaks and its valley depths in union with the new Adam.

"There was in Jerusalem a man named Simeon. He was an upright and devout man; he looked forward to Israel's comforting, and the Holy Spirit rested on him.

"It had been revealed to him by the Holy Spirit that he would not see death until he had set eyes on the Christ the Lord.

"Prompted by the Spirit, he came to the Temple" ... and when he saw the holy Child he took Him into his arms, as he said a prayer praising God.

Now, Master, You can let Your servant go in peace, just as You promised, because my eyes have seen the salvation which You have prepared for all the nations to see, a light to enlighten the pagans and the glory of Your people Israel. (Lk. 2:25-27, 28-32)

Mary and Joseph wondered at the man and his prayer. Was Simeon a priest like Zachary? He must have spent much time in prayer and close union with God to be able to hear and follow the promptings of the Spirit and recognize God's Son.

After his prayer, Simeon turned to Mary and Joseph, blessed them, and then looked at Mary. It must have been a searching look that pierced the future and sent cold chills through her.

"You see this Child," he said, "He is destined for the fall and for the rising of many in Israel, destined to be a sign that is rejected—and a sword shall pierce your own soul, too—so that the secret thoughts of many may be laid bare" (Lk. 2:34-35).

What mother, before or since, has ever heard such a prophecy? A prophecy that rang in her ears for the rest of her life.

It must have been terrifying to know that your child would cause people to make choices: some would accept Him and some would reject Him.

The world would be divided between the time before His birth and the time after.

Men would be divided as some were for Him and some against Him.

Belief in Him would separate mother from daughter, father from son, and brother from sister.

Each one that rejected Him would pierce her heart.

His hardships would distress her loving heart, for it would be one thing to read about His life in the Prophecies and quite another to experience every hurt and every pain.

She must have pondered his words often. Simeon said that secret thoughts would be laid bare.

This part had already begun, for Simeon himself revealed the secret of God's revelation to him. At the sight of the Child he readily spoke his hidden thoughts.

The evil thoughts of the Pharisees would be forced out by the holiness of the Lord's life. Everyone who met Him would be either for Him completely or totally against Him. No one would be indifferent.

No words will ever express her sorrow as she bore the indifference and rejection of His chosen people and the many weaknesses of His Apostles.

Although these pains and many others were in the future, for a terrifying moment she felt their shadow pass over her.

All this was predicted by an old priest to a young couple. But the Deceiver knew it not.

SUFFERING OF THE INNOCENT

It is recorded in St. Matthew that an Angel of the Lord appeared to Joseph in a dream and told him to get up and escape into Egypt because Herod intended to search for the Child and kill Him (Matt. 2:13).

Although the word "intends" indicated he was merely thinking about it, Joseph lost no time.

He woke Mary and the Child, took their few possessions, and went out into the darkness of the night towards Egypt.

As he traveled, Joseph must have thought how his life had changed since Nazareth. For years he had lived a quiet life of work and worship. Then Mary came along—Mary, the Promised Woman—and his life began to be lifted up to the heights and cast down to the depths.

It was no longer a complacent life. He was constantly making choices—choices that not only affected himself but the whole world.

And now, this choice—Yes, he would obey the Angel. He would take no chances.

It didn't matter that he went into a strange country, where it would be difficult to get work, to make friends, or to worship on the Sabbath.

He would not question God's Plan. He had learned in Bethlehem that God would provide for them. His only obligation was to follow His Will—God would take care of details.

But was he ever tempted during the journey through the desert to wonder if this was really God's Son—God's Son running from a tyrant? Could not the Father annihilate this enemy as He had done long ago in Egypt?

And what of Mary and the Child? The desert nights were so cold, only to be followed by boiling heat during the day; would they both survive?

Whether or not these thoughts crossed his mind, it is certain that his faith was stronger every time he looked upon the Mother and her Child.

When he was in their presence, all doubts seemed to blow away.

Yes, this was God's Son — sent by a Father who loved His creatures so much that He would make no exceptions for His Son.

The purpose of His coming was to redeem. To redeem means to buy back, but before He could buy, He had to earn — earn in the same way His fellow human beings had to earn — by tears, suffering, and the sweat of their brows.

It must have been doubly painful for Mary, because her holiness would make her more sensitive to the sufferings of others. She must have pressed the Child to her breast to keep Him warm at night, and shaded His tiny head with her veil during the day.

It was her strength and faith that overflowed into Joseph. Her humility was too deep to ever doubt God's Providence, but this did not ease the suffering of the journey.

In fact, the suffering of the journey was enhanced because her sensitive nature felt every pain of the Child and the mental anguish of Joseph. Yes, the Woman's portion would always be double.

The beautiful feminine nature that Eve had disfigured through pride and pleasure, the Woman would restore through humility and suffering.

She began to imitate Him as soon as He was born. He was innocent but suffered from the tyranny of evil men, and she would follow wherever He led.

The first Eve led the first Adam, but the second Adam led the second Eve.

The Holy Family were the first Innocents to suffer for the sake of the Kingdom, but there were more.

Secret thoughts began to reveal themselves, as Simeon had foretold.

As the Holy Family fled into Egypt, Herod sent his soldiers to Bethlehem and its surrounding district, and ordered them to kill every child two years and under.

To what depths of evil is man capable of falling! For the first time since His birth we have a picture of the two opposing kingdoms: the one, holy, pure, and innocent; the other, evil, degraded, and cunning; the one, seeking the glory of the next world, and the other, the glory of this world.

The Child was all too soon a sign of contradiction. He came to save, yet in making all men choose, some would be lost.

The soldiers followed Herod's orders and killed perhaps thirty or more children. What a terrifying event. Babes at the breast, and in cradles, were all suddenly snatched away from loving arms and brutally murdered.

We can look back and realize how privileged they were. They died that He might live, so that He in turn could die that all mankind might live.

But the parents of those children did not see the future or the purpose of this tragedy.

Perhaps there is a lesson for all of us in this incident. We must trust His Wisdom and Providence in all the heartaches and tragedies of life, even though we may see their purpose and benefit only in eternity.

The parents of these children must have received tremendous graces from the Father as their children became the new Kingdom's first martyrs. Yes, God would bring good out of evil.

One thing is certain, this massacre brought the coming of the Messiah to the attention of the entire populace.

But Herod's pride made him think he had destroyed the Messiah. And so again, the Deceiver was deceived.

A CHILD IS LOST

Scripture does not tell us how long the Holy Family remained in Egypt. It may have been a month or a year, but one night "an Angel of the Lord appeared to Joseph and said, 'Get up, take the Child and His Mother with you and go back to the land of Israel, for those who wanted to kill the Child are dead'" (Mt. 2:19-20).

When they arrived in Israel, Joseph learned that Archelaus had succeeded his father, Herod, and he was afraid.

It is beautiful to see the virtue of prudence in action. Joseph did not say, "We can go where we please because we have God's Son with us and He will protect us." No, he realized that God expects us to take every precaution to avoid evil even if sometimes it means going to another place.

Joseph would not presume, and so he used common sense and went to Galilee and settled in Nazareth.

They must have met their old friends who probably wondered where they were for so long. But in a short time they settled down to a very ordinary way of life—so ordinary that people hardly noticed them.

Joseph worked as a carpenter, and Mary did all the things a wife and mother did in those days—cooking, cleaning, spinning, and getting water at the well.

It is hard to imagine, and yet it must have been that Joseph showed Jesus how to fix a chair, saw wood, and deal with customers who sometimes praised but more often complained about their work.

They prayed together, worked together, and worshiped together, and so it was that one year they went to Jerusalem to celebrate the Passover. Upon their return home the boy Jesus stayed in Jerusalem and His parents did not know it.

On religious pilgrimages, men and women traveled in separate caravans and at dusk they would meet for the evening meal.

Mary must have thought the boy Jesus was with Joseph, and Joseph, no doubt, thought He was with Mary.

Only parents who have lost children, one way or another, can appreciate the terror and guilt Mary and Joseph must have felt.

What thoughts raced through Joseph's mind? The Father entrusted His only Son to his care! How could he be so negligent? Why didn't he make sure He was in the caravan? Fear and guilt gripped his soul as he looked into the tear-filled eyes of Mary.

And what did Mary think? Her only Love was gone. Did His enemies recognize Him and kill Him? Was He kidnaped by slave traders and sold into Egypt, as Joseph of old? Had she displeased God that He would take away her Son?

Whatever thoughts raced through their minds, they hurried back to Jerusalem to look for Him.

It took another day's journey to return to Jerusalem. Joseph took one section of the city and Mary another. They asked citizens and shopkeepers, friends and acquaintances—but no one had seen Him.

What fear and terror held their souls captive as they searched and searched for Him, only to meet at an appointed place alone.

Did Mary think of the sword Simeon foretold would pierce her soul?

Probably not—she was too concerned about Him.

Throughout the centuries, all the mothers who lost a child would find in Mary a woman who knows what it means.

All those striving for holiness and experiencing the purification of soul that comes from dryness would find in Mary an understanding heart. She knows what it is to be without Him.

All souls that felt abandoned by God would find in her an example of persevering love and trust.

It was evening, and the search would have to end until tomorrow.

On the third day at dawn they resumed their search and looked for the Child again in all the familiar places, but He was nowhere to be found.

Perhaps it was Joseph who decided to go to the Temple. Yes, the Temple—could He be there?

Their hearts must have throbbed as they neared its precincts—throbbed with a kind of intuition as they neared His Presence.

And there, in the midst of the Doctors, sat Jesus, listening and asking questions. Mary and Joseph stood there overjoyed and perplexed.

Why hadn't they thought of the Temple before? Was He there for three days? Was He hungry—and where did He sleep?

If these questions did not cross Mary's mind, one question did, and she soon asked it, "My Child, why have you done this to us? See how worried your father and I have been, looking for You" (Lk. 2:48).

At the Annunciation, she asked *how* she would conceive Him, and now she asked *why* she had lost Him.

Both times her question was prompted by her humility and desire to do God's Will.

At the Conception, she desired to remain a virgin, and her lowliness made her feel unworthy to be His mother.

Now that same lowliness made her wonder what she had done to lose Him.

The Child answered, "Why were you looking for Me? Did you not know that I must be busy with My Father's business?" (Lk. 2:49).

Jesus was telling her that His disappearance had nothing to do with either one of them. They must both understand that He came into the world to do the Father's work. To accomplish this, He must be free to follow the promptings of the Spirit at any time.

Scripture says they did not understand, but detachment is always hard to grasp, and this was the first of many lessons in this virtue.

He was to practice what He would one day preach; that he who prefers mother or father, brother or sister, to God, is not worthy of the Kingdom.

But to prove that He came to fulfill the Law and thereby honor His father and mother, Scripture says, "He went down with them and came to Nazareth, and lived under their authority" (Lk. 2:51).

As they guided Him, He taught them the greatest lesson of all—the Father's Love, and that the Father's Will must be preferred by both of them above everything and everyone in the whole world.

What humility for God Incarnate to be subject to two of His creatures and to lower Himself to a nature that grew "in wisdom, in stature, and in favor with God and men."

What does it mean, "He grew in wisdom?" As God, was He not Wisdom itself? Is there anything to be known that He did not know?

Yes, as God He never knew poverty, or pain, nor did He suffer from the jealousy of men. He never felt hatred; but now that He became Man, He grew in the experience of all the consequences of sin.

Before He came, we could say to Him, "How do You know what it is to suffer pain, separation, and disappointment? Have You ever been hungry or thirsty, cold or in need of a friend?"

Yes, we could have asked Him those questions—but no longer, for now He knows. Yes, He grew in wisdom and He accepted every moment and everything it brought as coming from His Father—and so, He grew in God's favor.

MOTHER AND WIDOW

After the finding of the boy Jesus in the Temple, Scripture is silent until the beginning of the Public Ministry.

Why is it so silent? Every moment of His Life is important to us and we know nothing of this span of time.

Only Mary knew all that He said and did during that time. We know that all the first-hand information in St. Luke's and St. Mathew's Gospels must have come from Mary herself. Who else would know those hidden secrets and events?

Then why did she not tell more? There can only be one answer: she told only those things concerning herself that gave glory to God, proved her Son's Divinity, and showed His Power as manifested in the lowly.

All the events that concerned her personally, manifested her holiness, or showed her dignity as Mother of the Divine Word, she kept hidden.

Scripture says it is good to keep the secrets of the King and she kept hers well.

The new Eve, unlike the first Eve, would never eclipse her God. She was His humble handmaid and her only joy was and is to see Him glorified.

She lived the words that John the Baptist would one day say, "He must increase but I must decrease" (Jn. 3:30).

These years were no doubt years of spiritual maturity for Mary.

We can see from her life thus far that she had moments of great joy and great pain.

- Though she drank to the dregs her cup of sorrow, she never faltered.
- Though she often pondered, she never questioned.
- Though she did not always understand, she never doubted.
- Though at times she was set aside, she never rebelled.

Of the Lord's life on earth, 91% was hidden, and of Mary's life, 97%. The Holy of Holies and "Nature's Solitary Boast" lived lives of deep prayer before great works. They would stay close to the Source of all good works and drink deep of the fountain of living waters—the Father.

Somewhere between the Lord's twelfth year and public ministry, Joseph must have died for he is not mentioned again in Scripture.

We cannot imagine a more blessed death as we see Jesus and Mary near his side at that moment. What peace filled his soul as he realized his time of parting had come. He was a faithful foster father and a loving spouse, and he longed to see the Father whose Son he had cared for with such love. But he must wait, for the gates of Heaven would not be open until the Promised One had broken their seals.

Mary's love for Jesus did not lessen her sense of loss after Joseph's death. Her love for Joseph was pure and detached but ardent. She loved him as one chosen by God to protect and care for herself and her Son.

Jesus took up the carpentry work and spoke to the villagers about the Messiah.

Jesus and Mary must have spent hours together talking about the Kingdom and the Father.

Why this hidden life when there was so much to do, so many people to heal, so many to feed, so many dying in abject poverty?

His chosen people were under the yoke of Rome and they were without a prophet.

How different is the Wisdom of God compared to men! If we were in His place, we would have gone to the Temple and enlightened the Doctors of the Law, healed all the sick, made social reforms, and written volumes for future generations.

But instead, the Lord of Heaven spent thirty years alone with His Mother doing common work and in union with the Father in prayer. It was necessary to spend so much time with His Mother because of her mission. Later, he would do the same with Peter, James, and John, who also had a special mission.

Peter as head of the Church, James as the first martyr, and John who lived the longest and wrote the most about His Divinity—these men saw Him transfigured, raise the daughter of Jairus, and suffer in the Garden of Agony.

If this were to be true of Apostles, how much more so for His mother who had so much to endure, so much to learn, and so much to give.

He must have taught her the Beatitudes, the New Commandment, and the Counsels. He must have directed her pure soul through all the pathways of the inner life so she would understand as others traveled its ways.

He must have explained the Scriptures so she would understand the value of suffering, for many swords would pierce her heart.

And perhaps the greatest suffering during this time was the realization that as each day passed, the time of the public ministry and separation drew closer.

There is hardly any suffering that a human being could have that the Promised Woman did not endure.

Her feelings must have been mixed throughout these years. She longed to see mankind redeemed but she dreaded to see all the prophecies fulfilled.

She lived in both dread and expectation of the future. Had not the power of God sustained her, surely her life would have ended, as her spirit died many deaths in anticipation.

Eve had brought upon us the consequences of sin, and Mary would learn from the new Adam how to transform misery into glory.

- To carry God's Son the Temple of her soul had to be pure.
- To be His Mother, that Temple had to be holy.
- To be the first fruit of His Redemption, she had to know pain.

- ❧ To be His disciple, she had to understand His message.
- ❧ To be a Martyr, she had to endure a thousand deaths.
- ❧ To be great before God, she had to be nothing before men.

And so to be the Promised Woman, she had to endure all things and be all things to all men, so that her Son might one day tell mankind, through John, "Behold thy Mother" (Jn. 19:27).

It is no wonder that Jesus took so much time to form His Masterpiece.

DETACHMENT

Jesus neared the age of thirty and Mary knew the time had come. Was it spring—the time of year when all things are new?

Whatever time it was, it must have been a heart-breaking day. Unlike other mothers, who do not know their son's future, Mary was too well versed in Scripture not to know, at least in a general way, what lay ahead of her Son.

She must have stood at the doorway, as she was one day to stand at the foot of the Cross—tall, unselfish, brave, and totally united to God's Will.

What did she do, now that Jesus was gone? It is probable that she spun and sewed to earn enough to keep her until the groundwork had been laid by her Son. And then, with many other women, she would follow Him until the last.

Jesus came to keep the Law and He would keep the Fourth Commandment perfectly. He would not neglect her even though He must be about His Father's business.

Throughout the centuries, many holy souls have been granted extraordinary gifts from God, called "charisms." One, among many, is a kind of keen intuition—a mind-picture of what may be happening miles away.

If Mary was to experience untold pain to be called the Mother of Sorrows then she also experienced untold mystical gifts to be called the Mother of Saints.

And so, there must have been times, until she joined Him, that she somehow knew where He was and what He was doing.

She must have known, as only those who love deeply know, when He was led by the Spirit to be tempted—and she prayed and fasted.

She must have felt some special grace as her only Love walked into the water to be baptized by John—and she marveled at His humility.

She must have felt a sudden, unexplainable joy in her soul when the Father thundered from Heaven and the Spirit hovered over His Head and the Voice said, "This is My beloved Son, my favor rests on Him"—and she praised God (Mt. 3:17).

She must have known the day He went about choosing His Apostles—and she prayed for each one of them.

Detachment

Three days after He chose His Apostles, He was invited to a wedding feast at Cana in Galilee, and His Mother was there (Jn. 2:1).

The celebration for a wedding was at least seven days, and with extra guests, the wine soon gave out.

The couple must have been poor, but even the poorest were always sure they had enough of everything for the wedding feast. And now—the wine was gone—it would be very humiliating for the young couple. The neighbors would laugh them to scorn.

Mary, in her loving heart, realized their embarrassment and looked at Jesus. As their eyes met, did she understand He wanted to help? Was He looking for a reason to manifest His Power to His newly formed band of disciples?

His miracles were always and only signs of His Sonship. How would He launch out on His mission of healing souls and bodies?

The Father told the serpent He would put enmity between his seed and the Woman's seed. It was time to begin.

Mary looked at Jesus and said, "They have no wine" (Jn. 2:3).

The great moment had arrived. Mary, too, began her mission, for Jesus looked at her and called her "Woman"—the name of all names — pronounced by the Son as it was once pronounced by the Father — a name He was to call her during His entire public life.

Her Seed would crush the head of the Deceiver — She was the Promised Woman. Only at His death would He refer to her as "Mother" and that in order to give her to us all.

But the Master had more to say, as He continued, "Why turn to me? My hour has not yet come" (Jn. 2:4).

Was she anticipating His hour of death by asking for a miracle? Everyone would surely know, or at least suspect, who He was, and then would begin the road of sorrow.

Was He saying now, as He would say in the Agony in the Garden, "Let this hour pass. Nevertheless not My Will but Thine be done" (Lk. 22:42)?

She was a valiant woman — a woman who knew that only the Father would decide the exact Hour His Mission would begin. The Father would tell them both if this were the time.

As it was through a man and a woman that mankind fell, it would be through God's own Son and His Mother's cooperation that the Redeemer would do the one thing that would proclaim Him Lord of Creation.

She looked at the servants and said, "Do whatever He tells you" (Jn. 2:5). She would not anticipate the hour but if it was the Father's Will, she wanted Him to know He had her *Fiat* now as He did thirty years ago.

"Be it done unto me according to Thy Will" (Lk. 1:38). "I willingly give my Son, to suffer and to die, and I will follow Him at a distance until He needs me."

There were six stone water jars there that had been used for ablutions. They were all empty, and each jar could hold anywhere between twenty to thirty gallons of water—a total capacity of 120 to 180 gallons.

Jesus looked at the jars and said to the servants, "Fill the jars with water," and they filled them to the brim. "Draw some out now," He told them, "and take it to the chief steward."

"The chief steward tasted the water, and it had been changed into wine." He tasted the wine, and called the bridegroom to ask him why he kept the good wine until last (Jn. 2:6-10).

It was customary to put out the very best wine the first day or so of the feast, and then cheaper wine toward the end.

Little did they realize that the best wine was just beginning to flow: the red wine of His Love and Sacrifice was to be a never-ending fountain of joy and strength for all those who would come to the marriage feast.

It was symbolic of the great holiness men would be called to. The water of their poor human nature, touched by His Grace, would be changed into the wine of Divinity; they would be, in truth, sons of God. Truly, the best wine was kept by the Father until now.

The Apostles were dumbfounded, but no more than they would be at another feast—a Passover Feast, when He would change wine into His Body and Blood. And they believed in Him from that moment. And Scripture says that "after this He went down to Capernaum *with His Mother* and the brothers, but they stayed there only a few days" (Jn. 2:12). From that day, too, the Apostles' mission began for they were now known as the brethren.

Mary began to travel with Him; always in the background with the other women, always putting herself in His shadow, following in His footsteps, listening to every word, and pondering them all in her heart.

She marveled at His Wisdom as He gave the Beatitudes— and followed them.

She admired His zeal as He drove the money-changers from the Temple and prayed for them.

She saw John the Baptist, whose birth she attended, proclaim her Son the Lamb of God, and she foresaw the slaughter.

She heard Him speak of His Father and the Spirit to come, and she praised God.

She saw Him cure the deaf, blind, lame, and lepers, and she thanked Him.

She saw Him humiliated by the proud Pharisees and Doctors of the Law, and she wept.

She saw Him seek the lost sheep and press them to His Heart, and she rejoiced.

She heard Him reveal the secret of the Trinity within us, and she bowed in adoration.

She saw Him follow the Law and imitated His obedience.

She heard Him one day finally tell His people, "before Abraham ever was, I Am," and then she cried, as they picked up stones to throw at Him (Jn. 8:58).

She saw Him raise the dead, and glorified God.

She saw Him cast out demons from sinners, and prayed they would not be possessed again.

She saw Him cry over Jerusalem because it did not know the time of its visitation, and she cried with Him.

She listened as He taught His disciples the mysteries of the Kingdom, and watched many of them walk away when He revealed the Sacrament of the Eucharist.

She shuddered as He revealed His suffering and death to His Apostles, and realized they did not understand.

She rejoiced when He told His disciples He would rise on the third day—only to realize they did not comprehend.

And then she knew it was over all too soon—and she prayed.

Twice it is written in Scripture that Mary and His followers—who were referred to as brothers and sisters of the Lord—were outside waiting for Him.

But when someone informed the Master, He told the crowds—and through them, all mankind—that all those who do His Father's Will are mother, sister, and brother to Him (Mt. 12:50; Lk. 8:21). But they did not understand.

It was only at the Last Supper discourse that the disciples understood what He meant, for He told them that when they kept His Father's word, He and the Father would come and make Their home in them.

Divine Adoption! Through the power of His Spirit, Grace would absorb our souls and we would be sons of God in truth.

As He had lived in her He would live in us and we would be His Mother. As His Blood flowed in us through the Eucharist, we would be His brother and sister.

But the people wondered what He meant and if she felt hurt, but the Promised Woman understood. She was to be given to us as Mother and we in turn would be her children. Through His Love we would all belong to each other.

And then one day the Father inspired a woman to cry out in the crowds that the Woman who bore Him was blessed—and again Jesus took the opportunity to declare publicly that what made her blessed was her perfect union with God's Will.

Yes, He would say, blessed are those who hear the Word of God and keep it (Lk. 11:27-28).

He was telling us to see beyond her being His Mother. We must see what made her the Promised Woman; her humility, her perfect love, her adherence to God's Will, even to sacrificing her Son for our salvation.

She was His Handmaid—an example of His teaching, a friend in need, a follower par excellence, and a companion in suffering. These are the things that made her Blessed—as they would one day make us blessed. And she was soon to show the world how blessed she was.

SACRIFICE

Eve *made* history by her pride and disobedience. It was the role of the Promised Woman to be an intimate *part* of history — salvation history — by her humility and obedience.

She lived hidden with Him in His hidden life; she stayed in the background during the glory of His public life; but she came forth in His hour of pain and humiliation, because she was the Mother of Humility.

Eve would put herself ahead of Adam in the Garden of Paradise, but was put below him in the valley of tears.

The Promised Woman would be hidden in the Garden of His Triumph, but came forward in His Garden of Agony.

The time for which He came and longed was upon them. Mary must have shuddered and given a sigh of relief.

The Shadow of the Cross had somehow clouded every triumph of His public life and every joy of the hidden life.

It was His last Passover Feast, and the crowds were wondering if He would appear. Everyone knew how much He was hated, and people from every nation, who were there to purify themselves, must have had some kind of intuition that their purification this year would somehow be different.

Everyone wanted to see Him. People from all nations had heard of Him, and their curiosity and enthusiasm knew no bounds.

Suddenly, one of the pilgrims saw Him and cried out, "Hosanna! Blessings on the King of Israel, who comes in the Name of the Lord!" Someone else cut down a Palm branch, and then it was as if an unseen force took hold of them and the entire crowd began to shout and cut off palm branches to throw in His path as He came into Jerusalem seated on a donkey (Mt. 21:8-9).

"Hosanna, Hosanna, Hosanna," they cried out. It was a moment of triumph—but, as it is with this world, it was only for a moment.

Mary's feelings must have been mixed: ecstatic joy that finally He was acknowledged for what He was—King of Israel, and profound sadness that these same people would make Him a Man of Sorrows!

How fickle human nature is, she thought—how unstable. Were they worth dying for? Yes, their very depravity needed a God to heal them, to change them, to make them new!

The hours and minutes of this new week seemed to pass so quickly. The Lord had arranged to have supper in a large upper room in the house of a believer. Although there is no account of Mary being there, who is to say she did not know, as other Saints were to know, the mysteries that were about to be revealed?

If St. Paul was to be wrapped into seventh heaven and understand mysteries that the human mind could not comprehend, who is to say that the Promised Woman had lesser gifts of perception?

And so she must have known the sentiments of His Heart as He knelt before His Apostles to wash their feet. What a price for pride, she thought—God kneeling before finite creatures that they may do likewise.

What love must have possessed her soul when her Son took bread, broke it, and said, "This is My Body"—took the cup and said, "This is My Blood" (Lk. 22:19, 20). Did she in some miraculous way receive that Precious Body and Blood? Was she not the first human being to carry her God in such an intimate way? If she were so full of grace that she was a worthy vessel for His Conception, how much more worthy was she now to receive His Body and Blood?

She had given Him hers when He needed it—He would give her His when she needed it.

Did she in that same mysterious way know when He entered the Garden of Agony? She was too united to Him all her life not to know, as all mothers know, when her Son was in torment.

Wherever she was, she did not sleep. Her mother's intuition kept her awake and aware of those three hours' agony, and she, too, agonized that she was not closer, to wipe away the bloody sweat from His brow. But this was His Hour—the Hour He longed for, and He must do it alone.

Something must have suddenly gripped her soul as she felt Him being taken prisoner, betrayed by one of His own. The thought must have crossed her mind, "If an enemy had done this, I could have borne it—but you, my friend and companion!"

As all the Apostles ran, John perhaps looked for her to tell her what she already knew—they arrested her Son and at this moment were dragging Him before Caiaphas.

John ran back to the Court and Mary and the women followed Him until the very last.

She could only catch a glimpse of Him here and there, but the humiliation and hurt on that Sacred Face wrenched her heart as though a thousand swords pierced her.

She closed her eyes and felt the pain and the insult as they spit in His Face and hit Him with their fists. The next time she caught a glimpse of Him, His Face was swollen from the blows, and she remembered it was written that there was no comeliness in Him (Is. 53:2).

As she stood outside the courtyard straining to see Him, did she hear Peter say, "I do not know the man"? Three times it rang in her ears; three times she prayed he would repent (Mt. 26:72).

And then, Our Lord, whose beautiful face was now disfigured, cast a glance at Peter — who went out and wept bitterly (Lk. 22:61-62).

Where was Jesus during the night? St. John says they brought Him before Pilate in the morning. Was He put in some dungeon and tormented all night? We will know only in eternity — but she knew and she prayed.

Jesus was sent to Pilate, and as He stood before him, did Mary have some ray of hope that perhaps this man might see through the jealousy of the Pharisees and release Him?

What an opportunity Pilate had! He could release his God from torment by an act of his will. An act of God's Will brought Pilate from nothingness into existence, and an act of Pilate's will brought his God from life to death.

The more Pilate questioned Jesus, the more he realized He was innocent. Perhaps Mary's prayer was being answered — Pilate was seeing through it all!

But ambition and human respect made Pilate take advantage of the opportunity, and so he sent Jesus to Herod.

How well Mary knew Herod and his father before him. Jesus would only be humiliated more, and so, in reparation, she kept glorifying His Divinity.

- For every act of hate, she loved.
- For every blow, she made reparation.
- For every insult, she knelt in adoration.
- He was without comfort, and she without consolation.
- He was without a friend, and she without a companion.
- He was hated by the crowds, and she was despised as His Mother.

 He was accounted as a criminal even by those He healed, and she would be cursed by His enemies.

Before Herod, Jesus was silent, and He was treated with contempt (Lk. 23:11). It must be so, for holiness has nothing to do with evil and Herod was evil.

When he was through playing games, he sent Jesus back to Pilate.

Perhaps that faint ray of hope welled up in Mary's heart again. Pilate saw the light—would he follow it?

Pilate was angry and frustrated as he saw Jesus returned to him. He felt uneasy about this Man. Why? He had condemned others without a pang of conscience. Why was this Man different?

He would question Him again. "Are You King of the Jews?" he asked. Jesus admitted the truth, but maintained His Kingdom was not of this world (Jn. 18:33-36).

Mary prayed as she never prayed before, while Pilate played with his decision. He would compromise. He would punish Him to satisfy jealousy and release Him to satisfy his conscience (Jn. 19:1).

Mary's heart sank for she realized that once one begins to compromise between the two Kingdoms, the Kingdom of darkness is ahead.

Pilate would scourge Him and let Him go. Who could describe her feelings as she saw them strip Him to the waist and tie Him to a pillar?

She had taken such care of that Body as an Infant, caressed it as a Child, adored it as a God-Man, and now beheld it being torn and bruised—for our sins. She felt every blow in her own body and every crack of the whip tore at her soul.

The Lord's patience and meekness were so sublime that all hell broke loose. The Deceiver would make this Man scream. Was He God's Son? No, he thought, God's Son would never be humiliated like this. How could He love sinners this much?

The devil's fury was unbounded and so he inspired the soldiers to plait a crown of thorns and put it on His Head. It pierced His brain and the Blood flowed—and Mary's eyes closed in terror (Jn. 19:2-4).

When they brought Him back to Pilate, He was "a worm and no man" (Ps. 22:6). Pilate stood Him before the crowd and said, "Behold the Man!" (Jn. 19:5). Surely, he thought, a man so torn and bruised would elicit some sympathy—this would be enough to placate their jealousy.

How could Mary look upon that disfigured Face, whose kindness had turned sinners to repentance; those Hands, now so swollen, that had once healed lepers; those Eyes, closed with dried Blood, that had read men's hearts?

Yes, she would look — look and adore. Her faith never failed, her courage never waned; though all fled, she stood firm.

Finally, the spirit of darkness took over Pilate. His vacillating will could no longer compromise. He tried not to make a choice: he scourged Him for no reason to placate their envy: he released Barabbas to force the final choice on them: but the time of his personal choice arrived, and as the crowds cried, "Crucify Him, Crucify Him," he made his own decision. To ease his conscience, he washed his hands before the crowd, and condemned Christ to death.

"Crucify Him!" — That cry of hate rang through Mary's ears like a thousand bells at close range. Where were all the blind, deaf, dumb, and lepers? Fear had gripped their souls and they ran, as His Apostles had run.

The more they cried "Crucify Him" the more her heart said, "Father, glorify Your Son: accept His ignominy for sinners and for all mankind." The great gifts she received and the Virgin Birth, she knew were all given her in anticipation of this time — the culmination of our Redemption.

As they placed the Cross upon His Shoulder and His Body sank beneath its weight, her heart was wrung with anguish. She watched as He fell again and again and wished she could lift its weight from His torn shoulders.

People jeered at Him and whispered as she passed them by, "They say that's His Mother; she is responsible for His delusions—why He thinks He is God's Son!"

She followed Him as if she did not hear the insults hurled at her.

What did it matter? The only thing that counted was Him. The soldiers kicked Him when He fell and she wondered if He would make it up the hill.

She whispered a prayer for help, and finally the soldiers, afraid He would not make it to Calvary, enlisted a man from Cyrene, called Simon, to help Him (Mt. 27:32).

And then they crucified Him. Every sound of the hammer as it struck the nails in His Hands and Feet, were felt by her own body. Surely it took special help from God, for Scripture says she *stood* beneath the Cross (Jn. 19:25).

She stood in full view—as the Mother of the Man of Sorrows—uniting her will to His Will, her pain to His pain, and her desolation to His desolation.

He spoke from the Cross of His abandonment and of His thirst for souls. He promised paradise to a thief (Lk. 23:43)—and then proclaimed her title and role to the world.

He looked down and saw her standing at His feet, and said, "Woman, this is your son" (Jn. 19:26).

Jesus declares to all mankind that Mary is the new Eve —she is the Promised Woman whose seed will in a few moments finish the blow that will crush the head of the Deceiver. He was also telling us He was her *only* Son—else why give her to John if He had brothers? He looked after her by giving her to us all.

Yes, she is the spiritual mother of all the faithful, as represented by John, for Jesus looked at him and said, "This is your Mother" (Jn. 19:27).

Adam and Eve stood for mankind, and failed, and with their failure we all failed.

Jesus on the Cross took their failure upon Himself and died that we might live.

The person who has never felt the love and warmth of a mother lives only half a life. As it is in the material world, so it is in the spiritual world. We need the warmth, friendship, and love of a mother.

The new Eve brought forth a Son who died for our sins. He gave every drop of His Blood for our salvation. He died in poverty, and when He saw the only possession He had left in the whole world—His Mother—He gave her to us.

Dispossessed of everything, He said, "It is finished" and commended His Spirit to the Father (Jn. 19:30).

He suffered three hours in the Garden, and three hours on the Cross. In His Hour of Reparation, was the number three significant?

Pride, the cause of our fall, dwells in all three faculties of our soul—memory, understanding, and will. It turns all past successes to ourselves and forgets all failures. It sees only its own good, and understands nothing that does not inflate its ego. Its will seeks only itself and its pleasure.

And so, perhaps, the Lord Jesus, for three hours, emptied His memory into the depths of desolation, purified His understanding by seeing the Father's Hand in every pain—so much so, that He could say, "Father, forgive them; they do not know what they do" (Lk. 23:34)—and united His Will to the Father's so perfectly that when He commended His Soul to the Father, our Redemption was accomplished.

And did not Mary do the same? Her memory ever sought lowliness at the remembrance of the great things God had done to her; her understanding accepted everything her Lord permitted or desired, without hesitation; and her will ever clung to His as the only source of her joy.

He bowed His Head and gave up His Spirit. Redemption was accomplished. It was over for Jesus, but not for Mary. The centurion took a spear and pierced the heart of God. From that Heart flowed the little Blood that was left, and with it, water (Jn. 19:34).

The Promised Woman stood tall for she alone felt the lance go through the Heart of her dead Son. It was truly finished.

The Messiah came, lived, and died, and as the earth quaked, the Temple veil was torn and the day turned into night.

The Deceiver knew with a certainty that He had been deceived by the Messiah's humility.

Joseph of Arimathea, Nicodemus, and John took the Body off the Cross and laid it in the arms of the Promised Woman.

Her seed had been crushed as it, in turn, crushed the serpent's head. Though she was frail, the same courage that made her stand at the foot of the Cross gave her the strength to hold His Body, torn and cold, to her warm heart.

He was born in a stranger's cave and buried in another man's tomb. He came with everything and received nothing and He died with nothing, only to receive everything.

Mary, whose faith shone brighter in the darkness, knew that her hope in His promise would soon be realized.

JOY

It was evening when Mary and a small band of followers began their way home. The events of the day were unbelievable. It was like seeing Hope itself dashed against the wall of despair, and crumbling to pieces.

But where was home? Jesus had not a place to lay His Head or to call His own. The ground was His bed and the sky His blanket for so long.

They would go where it all began—to the Upper Room. He had strengthened them there with His Precious Body and Blood—perhaps that is where they should meet and recall the day's events—events that baffled description or comparison.

Somehow, all the dispersed band of followers—Apostles and Disciples—began to find their way to that Upper Room.

They were overwhelmed at what had happened to Him and discouraged at the sight of their own cowardice.

And Peter—the crumbled Rock—what of him? He had fallen, but unlike Judas, he would not despair. It was too late to tell His Master he was sorry but he could tell His Master's Mother.

Yes, perhaps they all felt the need to tell someone who belonged to Him that they were sorry—sorry they ran—sorry they didn't defend Him—and sorry they didn't die with Him.

Yes, they would go to Mary—she would understand—she was so much like Jesus.

One by one they went to the Upper Room and threw themselves at her feet and buried their heads in her lap, as they wept the tears of regret.

Though her sorrow was deeper than theirs, she comforted each one with words of hope and forgiveness. She had needed them in her time of trial, but she understood. He had asked the Father to forgive them for they did not know what they were doing, and she too would forgive—and more—she would pour on their wounds the healing balm of understanding love.

Though they had ears, they did not hear when He told them He would rise on the third day—but she heard, heard and believed.

The Woman who had Faith strong enough to stand at the foot of the Cross also had the kind of Hope that gave her the assurance that the tomb would soon be empty. When the women went to anoint His Body, she did not go with them.

Scripture does not mention Jesus appearing to His Mother, but who can think even for a moment that He did not?

If He appeared to Magdalen, out of whom He cast seven devils, to Peter, who denied Him, to Thomas, who doubted Him, and to all the rest, who ran away in His time of need — how much more would He appear to the one who stood by Him to the last?

She would want that meeting hidden; it would serve no purpose. It was necessary that these other appearances be recorded, to manifest His Mercy to sinners. His meeting with her was not so much out of Mercy as a reward for bearing so much fruit under trying circumstances.

Who could describe that meeting! She must have been alone, when suddenly her soul knew the time had arrived for the Father to glorify His Son.

There in the dark tomb, a light shone brighter than the sun. The cold, mutilated, and dead Body of Jesus, wrapped in a winding sheet, suddenly rose — rose in a glorified state. The same Power that raised the dead and healed lepers, raised His Body—and He passed through the sealed tomb.

The choirs of Angels sang Hosannas, and chanted, "Christ is Risen, Alleluia." "All at once there was a violent earthquake, for an Angel of the Lord, descending from Heaven, came and rolled the stone away and sat on it" (Mt. 28:2).

Mary felt the earth quake, and she knew He had risen. Before another thought could pass her mind, there He was—standing tall, majestic, and glorified!

She ran into His Arms and was filled to overflowing with all the comfort she was deprived of during the past week. She had been faithful and He was grateful.

He would not tarry, for He wanted to show Himself to Mary Magdalen and the faithful women. They, too, stayed with Him to the last, and He would appear to them before His Apostles.

She understood, for it was time again for her to remain in the background. This was His day of Triumph—He is Lord of All—the great Conqueror and King of Glory.

Yes, He must go and show Himself to everyone who followed Him. He would seek them out on the way to Emmaus, appear in their midst in the Upper Room, and cook breakfast for them at the Sea of Tiberias.

Joy

She rejoiced as each one ran to her to tell her the good news, and she assured them they need never fear again. Their Master would live forever.

She praised God when she saw the radiant faces of Mary Magdalen and the faithful women.

She smiled as she heard the account of the disgruntled disciples going to Emmaus and how the Master held their eyes so that they had not recognized Him until He broke bread.

She glorified His Mercy when she saw the relieved face of Peter as he told her the Master had asked for only three acts of love for his threefold denial.

And then she thanked God when Thomas believed after he saw her Son's five Wounds.

Yes, that day had been a glorious day, but it was His Day, and she would once more retire to the background. But this time she would live in the light of His Resurrection.

MISSION

For forty days Jesus appeared to His followers, sometimes to the entire group and at other times to individuals. In the Acts, the name of James is mentioned as one the Master appeared to; he would need this personal appearance for he would join his Master in the not too distant future — the first Apostle to die as a martyr for the sake of the Kingdom.

How many hours of these forty days did He not spend with Mary? She was to remain in this valley of tears, so she would need more grace and more enlightenment.

- She would be a Mother to the Infant Church.
- She would pray for its followers as they witnessed to His Power among the people.
- She would spend hours in prayer and would intercede for its holiness and its growth.
- She would weep over its failings and rejoice over its victories.

- She would warn its leaders of danger and encourage them to persevere to the end.
- She would do battle with its invisible foes until it was strong enough to fight the good fight.
- She would listen to its leaders as they spoke of the pains and the joys of their missions.

And then she would be filled to overflowing with His Grace and would spread the perfume of Holiness everywhere she went.

Yes, she had much to do, and she would do it in the same hidden way she did everything else.

She would never forget the One who had done great things to her and her only desire was to see Him praised and glorified. She was always on hand when He needed her and always hidden when all went well.

The Infant Church was as small as her Son once was, and she would nourish it with the milk of her love and devotion.

The forty days were soon over and it was time for Him to enter the gates of Heaven as the King of Glory. The Apostles were told to set out for Galilee, and there they saw Him and fell down before Him.

It was then that they asked Him if He was going to restore the Kingdom of Israel (Acts 1:6.) How little they had learned!

They still found it difficult to accept the Messiah as a spiritual leader; they still desired a bread and butter leader. It is strange that Scripture says that upon coming to Galilee some "hesitated" when they saw Him. Were they taken back by the Resurrected Lord or disappointed in His Mission (Mt. 28:17)?

His answer to their question about the Kingdom was simple and blunt. He replied, "It is not for you to know times and dates that the Father has decided by His own authority, but you will receive power when the Holy Spirit comes on you, and then you will be my witnesses ... indeed to the ends of the earth" (Acts 1:7, 8).

He had told them at table just a few days before that they would be baptized with the Holy Spirit; and now, just before He left them, He said, "All authority in Heaven and on earth has been given to Me. Go, therefore, make disciples of all the Nations; baptize them in the name of the Father and of the Son and of the Holy Spirit, and teach them to observe all the Commands I *gave* you. And know I am with you always, yes, to the end of time" (Mt. 28:18-20).

Suddenly, He was lifted up out of their sight. We are not told how long they were there, but Angels in white appeared and asked why they were standing there looking into the sky.

Did they not understand that in the same way as He ascended He would one day return, and then they would have the kind of King they wanted—Majestic and Glorious?

Mary must have rejoiced at the graces Jesus had given to them and the promise of the Spirit to come. They would go to the Upper Room and pray.

FULFILLMENT

Scripture says they returned to Jerusalem full of joy and prayed in the Temple daily. At night they would assemble in the Upper Room and talk over the events of the last forty days.

They must have wondered and conjectured as to what would happen when the Spirit came. Mary would be silent—she experienced the Power of the Spirit over thirty-three years ago as He overshadowed her and she conceived God's Son. She was the Spouse of the Holy Spirit, and she waited with great longing.

As the Feast of Pentecost arrived they were assembled together and suddenly, around nine o'clock in the morning, the house in which they were, began to shake, and it was as if a great wind had come into the Upper Room (Acts 2:2).

Then they saw what seemed to them to be tongues of fire, and as their eyes were held in fascination, the tongues began to part and came to rest upon the head of each one present (Acts 2:3).

They were all filled with the Spirit of God. The Spirit had accomplished in them what He had accomplished in Mary: Jesus was born within them—they were new men—they were transformed into Jesus.

Isaiah had prophesied long ago that the Messiah would be filled with the Spirit of the Fear of the Lord, the Spirit of Piety, the Spirit of Fortitude, the Spirit of Counsel, the Spirit of Knowledge, the Spirit of Understanding, and the Spirit of Wisdom (Is. 11:1-2).

Jesus came, suffered, died, and rose—as the first of many brethren—that they might possess by grace what He possessed by nature—Divine Sonship. Because He was filled with these gifts, they would also be filled.

Now He was not only Lord of Heaven but Lord of their hearts. They were a temple in which God would continue to live on earth.

They would now possess His Gentleness and Mercy, His Patience and Forgiveness, His Love and Zeal, His Discernment and Insight, His Knowledge of hidden things and Poverty of Spirit, His Courage and Fortitude, His Ability to see the Father's Will in everything—and most wonderful of all, God would be their Father because He was His Father.

Everything Jesus said at the Last Supper became so clear. "Make your home in Me as I make Mine in you" (Jn. 15:4). "Love one another just as I have loved you" (Jn. 13:34).

Now they understood—understood how they would be able to love their neighbor as much as the Father loves the Son—in the Holy Spirit (Jn. 17:24).

The Spirit within them would . . .

- give them a childlike relationship with the Father by the Gift of Fear of the Lord;
- make them one heart and one mind by the Gift of Piety;
- bring to mind all the teachings of the Master by the Gift of Counsel;
- give them courage to suffer with joy by the Gift of Fortitude;
- detach them from worldly possessions by the Gift of Knowledge;
- give them light to understand the mysteries of God by the Gift of Understanding;
- and make them see everything and everyone through the Eyes of God by the Gift of Wisdom.

How Mary rejoiced to see so many—those present and those to come—filled with the Holy Spirit, transformed into Jesus, and giving glory to the Father.

Her Son had accomplished His work. He merited by His life, death, and resurrection a Divine Sonship for fallen mankind.

He promised that with Him in us we would bear fruit in plenty —fruit that would last, and we would do greater things than He did to glorify the Father and witness to the Power of His Spirit.

The Apostles, and many others who followed, healed the sick, raised the dead, and cast out demons, but these were only signs of their God-given Mission.

The greatest thing each one accomplished was to empty himself so completely that the Spirit of God could possess his soul and transform it into the image of Christ.

This is truly the greatest of all works, and how well Mary realized it. She was given many special gifts, graces, and prerogatives, but the greatest of them all was her transformation into Jesus. She emptied herself every moment of her life that the Spirit of the Lord might direct her every thought and every action.

Eve had filled herself with herself. The Promised Woman was filled only with the Holy Spirit, transformed into Jesus, and was a most obedient daughter of the Eternal Father.

CITY OF GOD

The most remarkable thing about Mary is that such an extraordinary woman would live such an ordinary life.

It was her humility that made her appear as any other woman, so much so that many throughout the centuries have refused to acknowledge God's gifts in her — as if these gifts came from herself or she did not possess them.

We deprive God of glory if we do not look at the Promised Woman and praise His Power for what it has wrought in her.

It is like a king who carves an image of himself in a large diamond and gives it to us to behold, but we refuse and throw it away because we think it is only glass.

The Father would have to create a woman who would be a fit dwelling place for His Son. By the fact that she was to give His Word flesh and blood she would have to be immaculate — never, even for a moment, would she be in the hands of the enemy.

As His Son was to be the perfect Man, so the Woman would have to be filled with grace—never offending Him, always seeking Him, ever an obedient daughter.

What a marvel He must create—a finite creature—a weak woman—but so pure and immaculate that His own Son would find a suitable dwelling in which to become Man.

We cannot conceive the holiness of God, and so we cannot conceive the necessity of such a Woman. But God is beyond man's understanding, and our lack of comprehension does not diminish the truth.

The Promised Woman must be as Eve was in the beginning—without sin. Like Eve, the Promised Woman must be created without sin.

She who was to bear the fruit of God must have as much and more than she who bore the fruit of her own will.

For what was to be born of Mary was "not of the flesh, or of the will of man, but of the Will of God" (Jn. 1:13).

Then her will must be ever united to God's Will for she was to bear the fruit of that Will.

She would be a peerless creature in whom God would find His pleasure.

Her love and will must be so one with God's that the Holy Spirit could overshadow her and she would conceive and bear a Son. That Son would be God's Son, for her total being was so absorbed in His love that the Temple in which He took His abode was like Heaven, for it was filled with God.

She would be His Mother for He made her so; she would be His Immaculate bridal chamber for He prepared it for Himself; she would be His vessel for He would live in her and take on the bone of her bone and flesh of her flesh and they would be as one.

Her life must be a perfect imitation of His: she would be humble, hidden, sorrowful, and afflicted, but she would also know the joys that have not entered the heart of man. She would be all things to all men that she might understand their failings, though she failed not — be compassionate with their falls, though she fell not — and follow in the Master's footsteps in order to experience all the sufferings that poor human nature is subject to.

She who was filled with grace, could stand beneath the Cross, for she had accepted its burden with the same love as her Son. She would give Him as He gave Himself, and she would give herself as He gave her to the world.

Who else would be a terror to the demon but the Promised Woman? She it was who would crush his head and confound his pride. If demons fled from Peter, Paul, and many other holy men and women throughout the centuries, how much more would they fly from her!

She would stand tall and unafraid as the dragon tried to crush the Infant Church her Son had founded. The Mother of its Head was near and would put around it the protective mantle of her holiness and the love of her heart.

She would intercede for its members until the day her Son would return and take all the faithful on earth to Himself.

Her role would ever be Daughter, Spouse, Mother, Intercessor, and Refuge of Sinners.

Who is to say then, that as she was the most faithful imitator of her Son, and God's purest creation, she would not be the first to reap the fruit of His Resurrection?

If Prophets like Elijah and Enoch walked with God and were seen no more, how much more would this Promised Woman —God's Masterpiece of Holiness among finite creatures—be raised into Heaven as the first fruits of His Resurrection?

It is recorded in Scripture that as the Master died, many of the dead rose from their graves (Mt. 27:51-53). It is not recorded that they returned. Were they, too, to accompany the Master to Heaven?

One thing we can be sure of—that the Woman promised in the beginning, who bore God's Son, suffered in His agony, and was filled with grace would not decay in a grave. No, she had been faithful and He was grateful. He would say to her, "Come, beloved of My Father, accept the Crown prepared for you from all Eternity" (Mt. 25:34).

> Now a great sign appeared in Heaven: a Woman adorned with the sun, standing on the moon, and with twelve stars on her head for a crown. She was pregnant, and in labor, crying aloud in the pangs of childbirth.
>
> [Then the dragon appeared and] its tail dragged a third of the stars from the sky and dropped them to earth. The dragon stopped in front of the Woman so he could eat it (the Child) as soon as it was born. The woman brought a male Child into the world, a Son who was to rule the nations—and the Child was taken straight up to God and to His Throne.

As soon as the dragon found himself thrown down to the earth, he sprang in pursuit of the Woman.... But the earth came to her rescue.

Then the dragon was enraged with the Woman and went away to make war on the rest of her children, that is, all who obey God's Commandments and bear witness for Jesus. (Rev. 12:1-2, 4-5, 13, 16, 17)

Blessed are you, by the Lord, the Most High God, above
    all women on earth. You are the Glory of Jerusalem,
You are the Joy of Israel,
You are the Honor of our people. (Jud. 13:18, 15:10)

THE DIVINE
PERSONALITY
OF JESUS

THE DIVINE PERSONALITY
OF JESUS

Each one of us sees Jesus in a different way. A man who has a temper and works to control it admires the gentleness of Jesus. It is the patient self-control of Jesus during explosive situations that he admires and tries to imitate.

It is the same with other weaknesses and frailties. We all look for that quality in Jesus that we need the most, and our concept of Jesus takes on that particular characteristic.

Looking at Jesus in this way is a part of Christian living. The imitation of Jesus in his daily life is to the Christian a privilege, a heritage, a challenge, a goal, an obligation, and a vocation.

It is easier to look at only one of His beautiful qualities, but when we do we run the risk of never seeing the whole of Christ. Our concept may become so one-sided that we may not be prudent in our practice of virtue.

If an occasion arose where just anger was in order, we might be silent, thinking only of the gentle Christ, and forgetting zeal for the Honor and Glory of the Father.

Jesus possessed the ability to adjust and adapt Himself to every situation. He was totally selfless, and thought only of the Father's Honor and Glory. Everything He accomplished or spoke of was for the Father. His Soul was immersed in the Father, and He kept Himself perfectly free interiorly.

Because of this, He had the insight to know the most perfect action to take in every situation.

There were times He was angry, and other times, gentle. He was impatient with the weak faith of His Apostles, and tolerant with sinners who had no faith. He preached detachment, and yet cried at the tomb of Lazarus.

He spoke eloquently of the Kingdom and its joys, but had the compassion to raise a man from the dead because his mother was a widow.

His life was not a contradiction; it was a perfect balance of virtue and love. He would speak softly in the dark of night to Nicodemus because the man possessed so many fears, but the next day He spoke openly in the Temple and lashed out at the Pharisees for their pride and hypocrisy.

He was gentle with children and caressed them, spoke in parables to people who could not understand the language of the Law, forgave sinners, healed the sick, and trained men to be apostles and ambassadors of God. He was all things to all men without compromise.

He brought mere men up to His level, but if they refused to rise to a higher life, He left them alone. He gave men hope, but never ceased to warn them about temptation and the Enemy. He demanded a total giving of self, and then promised a reward that was "pressed down and running over" (Lk. 6:38).

To one crowd, He would speak of Mercy, Hope, and Love, but to another He would lash out with words of condemnation and warning. No matter what His words to a crowd were meant to convey, Jesus never ceased to be in complete control of Himself and of the situation. He gave to each person and each situation what it needed, and then went His way to another person and situation.

Everyone who approached Jesus with any desire for goodness, received in abundance, and those who sought nothing received nothing.

One day when the crowds jostled Him back and forth, He stopped and asked His Apostles who touched Him. Peter was impatient and replied that the crowds were pressing in upon Him — everyone was touching Him.

Jesus was not speaking of a physical touch, but a spiritual one. A woman who had suffered from a hemorrhage for years thought that if she touched the hem of His garment she would be healed. She managed to touch it and she was healed. The moment she touched His garment, power went out from Him, and Jesus felt it leaving His Body (Lk. 8:46).

He asked who touched Him, and it is strange that only one admitted doing so. Many had touched Him and He felt no power leave Him, for all those who touched Him among the crowd felt nothing.

Only Jesus and the woman had an experience — Jesus felt power leave Him, and the woman felt power enter her body and heal her.

Jesus possessed what the woman needed to be whole again, and she sought Him out. She looked for that power in Him to make up for what she lacked, and her desire was fulfilled. He was to her a healer, for she was sick. To others, He was shepherd for they were stray sheep. To some He was Prophet, for they needed to know the Kingdom was at hand.

But most of all, He was The Son of God, and He came to experience the consequences of the curse the Father had put upon mankind when Adam and Eve disobeyed. He came to redeem them from that curse, and in so doing, He became all things to all men. He became a "Man of Sorrows" acquainted with weakness but never succumbing to it.

He wanted to tell us that He knew what it meant to suffer, bleed, be rejected, misunderstood, and hated. He wanted to do all the things He commanded us to do so we would find it easier to forgive, overcome, obey, and be humble.

Because He was God and experienced what it means to be human, He has merited for us the grace to possess the Divine. Through Grace, bestowed upon us by the Power of His Spirit, we are sons of God and heirs to the Kingdom.

He has redeemed us with the Father, showed us how to act like children of God during our earthly pilgrimage, opened the gates of Heaven, and then sent His Spirit to abide with us as Guide and Teacher.

His Life had many qualities and virtues for us to imitate. He did not come in an arrogant way to show us up as failures. He came as a humble and obedient servant to show us how to live. He told us to follow in His footsteps with courage from

His Spirit, and then He promised us that someday we would share in His Glory as we had shared in His Cross.

We must look at the Personality of Jesus and see Him under various circumstances not unlike our own—and then praise Him by imitating Him to the best of our ability.

HIS CHARISM

The ability to attract people is referred to as a Charism. Whenever Jesus appeared in public, He stood out in the crowd. It was something the average person could not explain—they only knew this Man was different. So different was He, that He seemed to divide a crowd into two distinct factions—those for and those against. No one ever met Jesus and went away unaffected. Few realized that before them stood God-made-Man. This divine quality set Him apart, and at the same time made Him approachable and understanding.

As Christians we often excuse ourselves and decry our lack of Charism in regard to people and the world. We seem to forget that Jesus merited for us this Charism—the Charism of Divine Love shining through a human nature.

He has given His Holy Spirit to each of us, that we might become by Grace, what He is by Nature—a son of God—Divine light shining through a human soul, Divine love radiating through a fragile vessel and giving light to all. As He stood before fishermen casting their nets, and said, "Follow Me and I will make you fishers of men," the sound of His Voice, and the look in His Eye, made them drop their nets and follow Him (Mk. 1:17).

These men were fascinated by the loving authority of a Master who asked and did not command, who loved first and waited for a return of love. This Man was a Master worth following, an unusual Man who called and chose, and yet left them free to respond.

The ability to ask and wait was a very winsome quality in Jesus. These men knew they could say "No," but His strong and loving request made them follow. They had to know more about One who could command in such a humble way. In their hearts they knew the choice they would make would be final, and from that moment on their lives would be different for having followed.

He never promised them greatness. He merely said they would do great things. Somehow, there was a difference and they knew it. Their greatness would come from following Him, and they were content. His Charism was enhanced by Truth for what He said came from the Father, and there was never any speculation in His words. He never left anyone wondering about the meaning of His Words, even though the things He said were often mysterious and difficult to accept.

His humble authority was like a magnet that drew the poor and repulsed the proud. The people of the streets could sit for hours as He taught them in terms they could understand. This, too, was something rare. He brought mysterious truths down to their level without the least sign of condescension. They felt one with Him. Even though He was above them, His humble dignity brought them up from the mud of depravity and permitted them to look at Him, not as an equal but as a Friend.

He never lost His dignity, but He never made others feel less for it. Every gesture gave them hope, and told them of His love and concern.

He stood as a man among men. His Dignity gave Him power to attract the multitudes, because He came to serve, and inspired others to serve as well.

As He went from place to place, throngs of people of every class ran to hear Him. He never lost sight of His Mission, though many hailed Him as a Prophet. He was Son, not Prophet, and His Charism shone forth with brilliance as He told believer and unbeliever alike that He was sent by the Father.

His Charism was never in danger from applause, and neither was it lessened by criticism. He held to what He was from God, and cared little for the respect of the "accepted" people of His day. He never doubted who He was or the purpose of His Mission, and this, too, astounded the crowds. When they picked up stones to throw at Him, He did not change His stand—He disappeared in the crowd and went to another town.

This characteristic aggravated His enemies and encouraged His followers, because He was unafraid of the opinions of men. It was a fascinating spectacle to see Him unshaken by the tricks and duplicity of the Pharisees and Scribes. This strength of purpose made His Charism even more attractive, for it showed the source of that Charism—the Father.

He never lost sight of His Mission to Redeem mankind. He never permitted ingratitude and hatred to weaken His determination to do the Father's Will and show forth His Love and Mercy.

In the midst of controversy as to His Divine Sonship, He stood tall and unwavering, and then merely asked His followers, "Who do *you* say that I am?" (Mark 8:29). He would tell them by word and deed, but He would not argue the point. If they did not recognize the Author of Truth, there was no need to say more. He would stand His ground, though all forsook Him, but He would accomplish His Mission.

He was a light in a dark world, and even though He knew that light would be a threat to some who preferred the darkness, He would continue to shine for all to see.

And this was His Charism. He was a Light sent from God —a Light that refused to be extinguished by evil. He never for a moment kept Himself from the Source of all Light. He gave His Light to others in a total and unselfish way.

His desire is that we, too, might shine in the world, determined, unafraid, and full of truth, with a sense of mission, giving Him to others as He has given the Father to us.

DETERMINED AND SINGLE-MINDED

We are all so conscious of the gentleness of Jesus that we tend to forget His great determination. It was at times demanding, but never overbearing. For example, He was determined not to use His Divine Power to alleviate any of His personal sufferings or problems.

We see Him fleeing into Egypt to escape the tyranny of an evil King whom He could have annihilated with an act of His Will. Instead, He would be as other men and suffer the consequences of jealousy and ambition.

He patiently waited until the King died before He returned to Nazareth, and then lived an ordinary life. It was so ordinary that He was looked upon as any other child of His day. When He was twelve, and Mary and Joseph brought Him to the Temple, He did not hesitate a moment to withdraw from them, even if by doing so He would cause them untold grief.

On the surface, this seems cruel, but in reality it manifests a determination to accomplish the Father's Will at any cost. It was time to plant the seed of His coming in the hearts of the leaders of His day, and He had to do it alone.

Though He was sympathetic with His Mother's grief, He was undaunted in His explanation that God's Will must be first in their lives (Lk. 2:49).

He was a Man who knew what He was about, and no person or thing would deter Him from doing what He was sent to do. If and when the time came to correct those in authority, He would do so no matter what personal risk was involved.

He ate with sinners and had compassion on the weak, knowing that such behavior aggravated the Pharisees and Scribes. Unlike John the Baptist, who castigated with words, He would lash out by actions and uncover the hypocrisy of His critics by questions that had no answers.

Some things He said with such determination that those who listened could hardly believe their ears. "Do not give dogs what is holy," He said, "and do not throw your pearls in front of pigs, or they may trample them and then turn on you and tear you to pieces" (Mt. 7:6).

Many Christians today think virtue should be a companion to evil for peaceful coexistence; Jesus, however, never left any doubt in the minds of His listeners as to His stand on sin.

He had compassion on the sinner, but His hatred of sin went so far as to make Him say a man who thinks adulterous thoughts has committed adultery. This is strange in the light of His treatment of the woman taken in adultery. "Has no-one condemned thee, woman?" "No-one, Lord," she replied. "Neither will I," He answered (Jn. 8:10-11).

How could He be so determined and so compassionate at the same time? The answer must be in the fact that He realized how strong the temptations of the Enemy can be, and how much the Enemy hates every human being. He understood how difficult it is for poor, fallen human nature to overcome the onslaughts of a superior intelligence. He saw sin for what it was—a lie and a rejection of God as Father and Lord. He saw the deception behind every sin and temptation, and He had compassion on the sinner, but He never condoned his sin.

He was determined never to compromise the two Kingdoms, and He knew of what we were made. Therefore, He could look upon sin with Divine vengeance, and upon the sinner with Divine Mercy.

He wanted His followers to have the same spirit of determination as He. One day when He saw great crowds all around Him, He gave orders to leave for the other side of the sea. One of His disciples said to Him, "Sir, let me go and bury my father first." But Jesus replied, "Follow Me, and leave the dead to bury their dead" (Mt. 8:21-22). Was the disciple the son of a Pharisee or Scribe, whom the Lord had described as whitened sepulchers, full of dead men's bones? If so, it would be better for him to let these spiritually dead men bury his father while he followed the Master. Great detachment is needed to follow a man of determination. Whenever the test of loyalty came, he would be asked to put his hand to the plow and not look back, for if he did, he would not be worthy of the Kingdom of Heaven (Lk. 9:62).

A marvelous quality Jesus possessed was His ability to maintain this spirit of determination in the face of failure and contradiction. He knew the things He said and did would separate father from son and mother from daughter, but this knowledge did not deter Him from saying what He had to say and doing what He had to do. He went so far as to say that unless we took up our cross and followed Him we would not be worthy of Him (Mt. 10:38).

Yes, He could tell His followers that the Kingdom of Heaven was "like a merchant who found a pearl of great price and sold everything he had to purchase it" (Mt. 13:45-46). A man must have a sense of priorities and be willing and determined to sell all and give all to arrive at the goal God has set for him. It takes great will power and that is the essence of determination—the will to be like Jesus, no matter what the cost. We see His entire life as a reaching out to see and do the Father's Will: searching for the sinner, castigating sin, manifesting compassion for the sick, and being an image of the invisible God. Everything else would come and go, but He would never swerve from this purpose and mission.

PERSONAL CONCERN

One of the most attractive characteristics of Jesus was His caring solicitude for everyone in need. This may seem a strange statement until we realize that a proud man is seldom in need; he is sufficient unto himself and whatever help he does receive is accepted as his due rather than an expression of concern and care. So it was that Jesus could not work miracles in His own town, nor enlighten the minds of the Pharisees and Scribes. They felt no need of Him and when there is no need there can be no solicitude or caring.

He Himself said one day that He came for the sick and not the healthy. He came for sinners and not the virtuous. Jesus was certainly not ignoring the healthy or virtuous but they were not in need and He came for all those whose lack of virtue or health needed His care.

His concern for the sick was never on a wholesale basis. He healed by looking at them, touching them, and speaking to them. Each one felt the Master cared for him in a special way. Even the ten lepers were cured on an individual basis, else there was no need to ask why the other nine did not return to give thanks?

One day when He went to the house of Peter and Andrew He learned that Peter's mother-in-law was in bed with fever. He went to her and took her by the hand and helped her up. How awesome is this scene in its simplicity! God gently takes one of His creatures by the hand and cures a fever. It was a personal concern that prompted Him and a thoughtful solicitude that helped her out of bed (Mk. 1:29-31).

As Jesus came down the mountain one day a leper approached Him. The crowd pulled back for fear of becoming unclean. Certainly Jesus had the power to cure him from a distance but He would not. He went up to the leper, stretched out His hand and touched him. That touch was personal. The leper felt he was Jesus' only concern, and he experienced an increase of love and faith (Mt. 8:1-4).

Scripture repeatedly uses the expression "stretched out His hand." It indicates a quality in Jesus we often forget. Those who were ill were mostly the poor, and because they were both poor and sick they would kneel or sit before the Master in an attitude of humble petition. They were often afraid and needed assurance. Jesus always made the first gesture. He always made a special effort to let these people know He wanted to help them. He wanted to touch them. He would not cure with an act of His Will alone. No, He would stretch His Hand over the crowd so those who needed Him would forever feel the touch of their God healing their pain-wracked bodies.

They would know their Lord had a personal interest in everything they did and in everything that affected them.

We see this beautiful quality when Jesus raised the daughter of Jairus. The child was dead and Jesus went into the room and took her by the hand and said, "Little girl, I tell you to get up" (Mk. 5:41). This was not the first time Jesus raised someone from the dead but there is a special thoughtfulness in this account. Everyone was so astonished to see the child come back from the dead they forgot how weakened her condition was. Jesus did not forget, for the One who called her soul forth in death knew only too well her physical needs. He told them to give the child something to eat. It is difficult for us to realize God would love us enough to care for those small details in our lives which we think unimportant.

How many of us feel that God is not interested in small things like our work, the weather, toothaches, parking places, and traffic lights? There is ample proof in the Gospels of Jesus' interest in small details — details that are not really important for salvation, but important for the comfort and consolation of the creatures He loves so much.

We see this attentiveness at the sea of Tiberias. The Apostles had gone fishing after the Resurrection, and at dawn they saw the Lord on the shore. He had prepared a charcoal fire with some fish cooking on it and loaves of fresh bread. Jesus said to them, "Come, and have breakfast" (Jn. 21:12).

God cooked breakfast for weary, discouraged, and not too faithful Apostles. With the exception of John, these men, who labored all night and caught nothing, ran away when their Master needed them the most. They loved much but their weaknesses deterred them from expressing that love when there was a choice to make. Yes, these were the men for whom God cooked breakfast with such loving solicitude.

How many of us would have gone to that trouble? How many would have thought it below their dignity to manifest this concern, assuming the role of a servant?

There is an incident in the Gospel of St. Mark that also shows the personal concern of Jesus for the human needs of His creatures. He spoke so eloquently of the Kingdom that a large crowd of more than five thousand followed Him and listened for three days without eating.

The Apostles were tired and wanted the crowd to go home. They were so hungry themselves that they were actually unconcerned about the needs of the importunate crowd but Jesus cared—cared for each hungry human being in that crowd. "I feel sorry for all these people," He said, "they have been with Me for three days now and have nothing to eat. If I send them off home hungry, they will collapse on the way, for some have come a great distance" (Mark 8:2-3).

For some people, three days of fasting would not be strenuous, and Jesus Himself fasted for forty days, but His loving Heart did not expect others to do what He did. Although He knew some would be able to arrive home safely, He knew most would not, and He had a personal concern for each one.

All through the New Testament, one has the awareness of Jesus looking at each person in a crowd as if he or she were the only one there. Each one healed, was touched by Jesus.

Each Apostle was chosen and treated on an individual basis. When they argued as to which was the greater, He was disappointed. He had treated each one with great love and that should have been sufficient for them.

And so it is in our individual lives. Though our lives and example influence many, each one of us is known and loved by Jesus on an individual basis. He deeply cares now, as He did then, for each man, woman, and child He created. No detail escapes His eye, no need is too small, no petition too great. Most important of all, He has *time* for each one of us—all the time we need to express our cares, to manifest our love, to repent of our sins, and to praise Him for His Goodness.

He gave of His time, and that, perhaps, is the most difficult thing for us to give to others. This is surprising in the light of how much time we waste or kill for want of something to do. We don't mind giving people "things" but when they need our time we find all kinds of excuses. This is the cause of much impatience on our part. We subconsciously allot a certain time for everything and everyone, and when they encroach on that allotment, we manifest signs of impatience.

We can see ourselves in the attitude of the Apostles, who constantly chided the Master for giving too much time to the people, children, and sinners.

This ability to take time with each person gave Jesus that something special that attracted the crowds to Him. It was so unusual to see a Master in Israel give his time lovingly, whole-heartedly, completely, and without hurry. It was a rare quality, and one that we as Christians must try to acquire.

In every human being Jesus saw the image of His Father, the power of His Omnipotence, the manifestation of His Mercy, and a soul reaching out for freedom and redemption. He felt sorry for them and gave His life, His pain, His suffering, His love, and His time, that they might understand the Love and Compassion of His Father.

ENERGETIC AND ZEALOUS

We don't often think of Jesus as being energetic. We have mental pictures of Him walking slowly down dusty roads, stopping here and there to chat with passers-by. We imagine His speech as being rather slow and deliberate, and we base this conception on the statement He once made about our rendering an account of every idle word (Mt. 12:36).

This is not the Jesus the Gospels portray. In order to spark enthusiasm, one must be enthusiastic, and Jesus inspired men to leave all things and follow Him *immediately*. Peter and Andrew left their boats, James and John their nets, and Matthew his money table. They left everything quickly, as if they sensed an urgency that would not wait for the least sign of hesitation.

Throughout His public life Jesus was constantly on the go, not hurried, but ever moving towards His goal — Redemption — by tirelessly reaching out to preach the Good News and heal the sick.

One day a Scribe approached Him and said He wanted to go wherever Jesus went. Jesus told him He did not have a place to go; foxes and birds had more than He, and in order to follow Him one must be so energetic for the Kingdom that everything else was secondary (Mt. 8:20).

Over and over again, we read that after He had preached all day to a large crowd, He would tell His Apostles they must go to the other side of the sea and bring the Good News to more people. His zeal knew no bounds. He would go to the limits of His endurance to tell them the Good News.

His zeal, however, was mixed with prudence, for there were other times when He would tell His Apostles they must go to some lonely place and rest awhile (Mk. 6:31). One day when they found such a place, the people anticipated their move and reached the haven before them. Jesus at once took pity on them "because they were like sheep without a shepherd" (Mk. 6:34). He forgot Himself and His fatigue and preached to the crowd late into the night.

The secret of His energy did not lie in a drive for personal glory or gain. His energy and zeal were the fruit of His love for the Father and for men. This is why He could maintain His zeal no matter what the opposition. His love drove Him to any length as long as He knew that what He did glorified the Father and contributed toward our salvation.

This is the reason He could castigate the proud Pharisees and Scribes. He had to tell them how deceitful they were. This was not only for their own sake but for the sake of the poor, who held them in high esteem, when in reality they were wicked shepherds with no concern for their sheep.

He had the detachment necessary to be zealous and energetic without being imprudent. He knew when to correct and when to have compassion, when to go to the limit of His endurance, and when to rest. His zeal was always for the Father's honor and glory, and His energy was used to love His Father with His whole heart, soul, mind, and strength.

He pronounced seven woes on the Pharisees with a vehemence that sent shivers through the crowd. His Apostles reminded Him that His words were antagonistic but He was undaunted and told them they were to bear greater fruit than the Pharisees or they would never enter the Kingdom.

Some in the crowd applauded Jesus for His stand against the hypocrisy of these men, but Jesus was not influenced by their approval. He did not find fault with some to please others. He was a light in the world and He came to give light. His kind of light was that by which a man could judge himself and see how to improve his life, his circumstances, his work, and his world. If that light brought out glaring faults and secret sins and made Him unpopular, His Heart would cry for their callousness. His Spirit, however, would continue to shine for all those who wished to bask in its Light. Every day He went to the Temple. Every day His soul was enraged by the profiteering of those leaders who should have been concerned for the spiritual welfare of God's People.

It was necessary to sell the animals used for the sacrifices and to exchange foreign money for the coin of the realm. This was not the reason Jesus made a whip from cords and drove these money changers away. These men had encroached upon the very precincts of the Temple. The Temple of the Lord was the House of His Father — a place of prayer, repentance, thanksgiving, and praise. The noise of animals, the cries of hucksters buying and selling, and the greed of crafty money changers clanging coins and cheating unsuspecting foreigners, overwhelmed Jesus with justifiable anger. If these transactions had to be made, they must be made elsewhere.

"He drove them all out of the Temple, cattle and sheep as well, scattered the money changers' coins, knocked their tables over, and said to the pigeon sellers, 'Take all this out of here and stop turning My Father's House into a market'" (Jn. 2:15-16). It is remarkable to see justifiable anger in action. In His zeal for His Father's honor and glory, Jesus had no human respect or fear. This did not make Him crude, cruel, thoughtless, or ruthless. His anger was not sparked by any personal injury, but only at the indignity, lukewarmness, and neglect shown in His Father's House.

One day He was to say, "As for human approval, this means nothing to Me" (Jn. 5:41). Jesus was free to do what the Father wanted Him to do, and to be what the Father wanted Him to be. He would not compromise for the sake of popularity or personal glory. He would be energetic without losing His self-control, and zealous without being overbearing. His two loves—His Father and Mankind—would be the determining factor in everything He said and did.

LOYAL

One of the most outstanding features of the Personality of Jesus was His Loyalty. He was loyal to His Apostles with full knowledge of their cowardice. He was loyal to the poor, accepting the criticism of the Pharisees so the destitute would never feel deserted.

He was loyal to His commitment, no matter how unpopular He became with the men of His time, and He was loyal to His Father, accomplishing His Will even unto death.

Yes, Jesus showed His loyalty in many little ways. One Sabbath day He took a walk through the corn fields and His disciples began to pick ears of corn and eat them (Mt. 12:1-8). The Pharisees seized the opportunity to criticize these simple men, but Jesus rose to their defense.

He saw through the Pharisees' hypocrisy and reminded them that He was Lord of the Sabbath. Their own priests did not violate the Holy Day as they worked in the Temple; neither did the Apostles break the Law by eating corn. They were with the One who was greater than the Temple, the Son of God.

The Pharisees would never understand loyalty because they used the Law and the people to suit their own purposes. They took advantage of every opportunity to criticize the poor and the lowly because in some way it made them feel important and better than the rest of men.

To them Jesus said, "If you had understood the meaning of the words, 'What I want is Mercy, not sacrifice,' you would not have condemned the blameless."

Exterior perfection is easier to attain than interior perfection. To give of one's goods, and keep the Law, can make a person proud and critical. We have a tendency to judge others by ourselves, and when they do not come up to our expectations or ideas of holiness, we are often hard and merciless.

Jesus was telling us that the virtues of compassion and mercy are more pleasing to Him than the material things we offer Him.

Jesus understood His Apostles in a way that is difficult for us to comprehend. These men were crude, uneducated fishermen. They were accustomed to rough work and frugal living. They were blunt, forward, and tactless. They showed impatience with crowds, were ambitious for high positions, and tried in every way to evade suffering. Our Lord's Loyalty made Him excuse and correct them with gentleness and patience.

When He found them arguing about their rank, He merely explained that those who served would be the leaders, and those who were last in this world would be first in the Kingdom.

The weaknesses and eccentricities inherent to their personalities and temperaments would not be an occasion for constant corrections. Jesus would wait until they were alone or the opportune moment arrived—that moment when they would reap the most fruit for their souls.

One day Peter was approached by a Temple tax collector, who asked him if the Master paid the half-shekel. Peter answered "yes" and proceeded to go into the house to ask Jesus for the money. The half-shekel was a tax imposed upon every Jew to support the Temple of the Lord.

Peter believed that Jesus was the Messiah, and one wonders why he felt Jesus would pay a tax for the Temple of His Father. Jesus also wondered because before Peter could speak, He said, "Simon, what is your opinion? From whom do the kings of the earth take toll or tribute, from their sons or from foreigners?" (Mt. 17:24-27).

Peter hesitated and then replied, "From foreigners." "Well then," Jesus said, "the sons are exempt." At this point, Jesus could have sent Peter back to the collector with an emphatic "No, my Master does not pay the tax; He is the Lord of the Temple," but the loyal and noble Heart of Jesus would not embarrass him.

After a pause that seemed like an eternity, Jesus answered, "So as not to offend these people, go to the lake and cast a hook; take the first fish that bites, open its mouth, and there you will find a shekel; take it and give it to them for me and for you." Jesus wanted to increase Peter's faith. This was only one of many little incidents in their lives together that showed Peter's weak faith. Jesus had to impress upon the mind of Peter that He was God's Son, and was not obliged to pay tax to Himself. However, since Peter's impetuosity had put them in an embarrassing position, Jesus paid the tax for both of them.

The finding of a shekel in the mouth of a fish was certainly a miraculous occurrence, but that miracle would not be brought about without some effort on the part of Peter. He had to go out to the sea, bait a hook, and wait for the first bite. This gave him time to ponder a little on the Divinity of His Master.

Only God would know what fish had swallowed a shekel, and only God could summon that fish to Peter's hook. Peter had another gentle lesson in Faith, and another example of the necessity of effort to increase that Faith.

Jesus could have asked Judas to pay the tax for Him, since he was the Apostolic treasurer, but He would not miss this opportunity to indelibly impress upon the minds of His Apostles and us, that He, Jesus, was and is God's only begotten Son, Lord of the Temple, King of Men, and Eternal God.

This is our faith — that Jesus is Lord and God. As impressed as the people were over His miracles, they did not realize His Divine origin. They were accustomed to Jewish healers and exorcists, and this miraculous power was always attributed to Prophets and other men sent by God to deliver Israel from her enemies. It was necessary for Jesus to keep His Divinity before their eyes.

Once, when He was questioned by the Pharisees, He told them, "Before Abraham came to be, I Am" (Jn. 8:58). Peter and each Christian after him must never forget that truth.

Jesus was loyal to an heroic degree, especially in two incidents during His life. The first in regard to Peter and the other Judas. Jesus made Peter the leader of His Apostles, the rock of His Church. No one would have condemned Him for taking that office away after Peter's threefold denial. Such an action would seem necessary and justifiable. However, the loyal Heart of Jesus realized that once this man was converted and grounded in a deep faith, he would be a beautiful example of the power of the Spirit and the Merciful Love of God. Though Peter denied Jesus, Jesus would never deny Peter.

It was the same with Judas. At least twice, Jesus told His Apostles that one of them would betray Him, but He never mentioned a name. When Peter asked John to inquire, Jesus merely said it was the one to whom He gave a piece of bread. Even in the Garden of Olives, Jesus looked at Judas as he approached to kiss Him, and said, "Friend."

The disgruntled disciples going to Emmaus were little deserving of loyalty. Jesus knew their hearts and understood their weak faith. He walked alongside and explained the Scriptures, and then broke bread to let them feel His Compassionate Love. He would be loyal while they complained and grumbled.

The loyal Heart of Jesus corrects with gentleness, teaches with patience, and forgives with love.

APPROACHABLE
AND AVAILABLE

When John the Baptist sent his disciples to ask the Master if He were the one who was to come, Jesus replied, "Tell John — the blind see again, the lame walk, lepers are cleansed, and the deaf hear, and the dead are raised to life, and the Good News is proclaimed to the poor" (Mt. 11:4-5).

Jesus made Himself available to everyone. Unlike former Prophets and the religious men of His day, who often kept themselves aloof, Jesus was easy to approach and always ready to give His help. He was never too busy or too tired to bless little children, touch a leper, or preach to those who longed for God's Word.

He was always at the right place at the right time. Lepers cried out to Him and were never afraid to reach out. For some strange, unexplainable reason they always felt they could approach Him and He would not turn away.

Little children ran to Him and crowded around His knees to ask for a blessing and hope for a tender caress.

Most of all, sinners felt attracted to Him. It was a phenomenon they could not explain. Infinite Holiness made Himself available and approachable to sinful creatures, whose souls were grotesque to behold.

Somehow, in the depths of their degradation, they knew they must get as close to Him as possible. As a flower turns toward the sun seeking warmth, these sinners sought the One who could restore their innocence and purity. They were never disappointed. He would look at them with great love and all the things that seemed so important to them would suddenly turn to straw. They knew they must change and follow Him.

No one ever imagined God would be so very close, so easy to approach, so ready to listen, and so lovingly forgiving. People had read about holy men, and they had seen John the Baptist, a Prophet of the Lord, but none of them were like this Man—the Son of God.

His eyes seemed to say to each individual, "Come to Me, and you will find peace for your souls." The touch of His hand sent healing powers through their bodies, exalted their souls, and made them seek only the Kingdom.

He was simple to talk to, and He listened to each one as if He had nothing else to do. They never felt rushed in His Presence. There was a strange feeling of time never ending when they spoke to Him. The Eternity He left seemed to extend itself and make them forget time, place, occupation, and their very selves.

They desired to drink in every word He said because those words burned in their hearts and lingered on to keep His Presence with them. His words were different from any other they had heard. No matter where they went after they left Him, His love and desire to forgive made them look upon their weaknesses as something that had to change. They must be like Him in every way.

One day Zacchaeus, the head of the tax collectors, ran to see Jesus. He climbed a sycamore tree in the hope of getting a better look at this gentle Messiah—a Messiah who sought out sinners (Lk. 19:1-10).

Zacchaeus was content to catch a glimpse of Him, but in his heart he wished and longed to be near Jesus—maybe even touch His garment. It seemed so impossible. He was the leader among tax collectors and he was merely tolerated by the Romans, and hated by the Jews. Such a holy Man as Jesus would certainly not be seen in his company.

As Zacchaeus mused within himself, he suddenly heard a voice say, "Zacchaeus, come down. Hurry, because I must stay at your house today." When sinners did not approach Jesus, He approached them. The Divine Mind that read the thoughts of all men, searched the heart of Zacchaeus and found it thirsting for God and He was there to give Zacchaeus a drink from the fountain of living waters.

Jesus gave us the parable of the Prodigal Son so we would never forget how approachable God is to His repentant children (Lk. 15:11-32). He depicts Himself as the father of an ungrateful son. The son squanders his inheritance and degrades himself to the level of an animal. But the father never stops looking for his son's return. He never tires waiting at the gate to be sure he will not miss him should he pass by.

There is no scene in Scripture as heart-warming as this parable that depicts how very approachable and available God is to poor sinners.

All during His life He desired to be with those who needed Him. He wanted to be available when the moment of repentance arrived. They did not have to wonder where to find Him.

He would search them out and patiently wait until they reached out for His Hand.

One day He told the crowds He was the Good Shepherd—the Shepherd who protected His flock, grazed it in rich pastures, and went after the lambs when they strayed from the fold (Jn. 10:11-18). He cared for them, and would always be available to help, to listen, to nourish, and to love.

NOBLE AND GENEROUS

We are generous when we give, but we are noble when we share and efface ourselves so others receive the glory.

Jesus was generous with His gifts and His power, but His Love was so great He shared His gifts and power with finite men.

He gave His Apostles the power to heal, cast out demons, and raise the dead, and He rejoiced when they returned to recount their deeds—deeds that *His* power in them performed.

He thanked the Father for sharing His gifts with men. He encouraged them to go out and use those gifts realizing that attention would be drawn away from Himself and given to them.

They had received these gifts freely and they were to give freely. They were to give the credit for their miraculous powers to God, and use the Name of Jesus to assure others of the source of these powers. The power in them would prove Jesus was sent by the Father — the Father who loved them so much.

During the Last Supper discourse, Jesus told His Apostles that whoever believed in Him would perform greater works than He did. He found pleasure in letting others share in the marvelous power He possessed as God (Jn. 14:12).

Only a generous heart would desire to give everything to others. Only a noble heart would share its power to perform miracles and reward His creatures for merely using the talents and gifts He gave them.

The entire life of Jesus is an act of generosity and nobility. He is the source of all goodness, and yet He rewards us for using the talents that are the fruit of His Goodness.

He never counted the cost of showing His love for us. He would warn the Apostles of future failings and then correct them gently after their failure to respond to His warning.

He never tired of giving examples of the kind of generosity He expects from us. When He gave us the parable of the Good Samaritan, He stressed the point of the man's generosity (Lk. 10:25-37).

Not only was the Samaritan a good neighbor by stopping to take care of the injured man's wounds. He brought him to an inn and paid the innkeeper to continue caring for him. He went even further. If it took more than he anticipated, he would repay the innkeeper on his return.

Jesus spent every moment of His life manifesting His love for the Father and mankind. He never seemed to think of Himself or His comfort. He healed as a sign of the Father's power in Him.

He spoke to the crowds to reveal the secrets of the Kingdom. He ate, drank, and slept to experience the needs of those He created. He suffered, bled, and died to give us courage and strength in our hour of trial. He rose and ascended into Heaven to give us hope and the opportunity to enter the Kingdom.

Everything He did was done for us out of love for His Father. He effaced Himself and was obedient unto death out of love, in one beautiful act of total giving and unselfish sharing.

He was Son of God and He desired that we be heirs to the Kingdom no matter what the cost. When the final hour came and He gave His soul back to the Father, there remained one last drop of Blood and a little water. It was like an unfinished symphony, the completion of which needed the note of one instrument.

The centurion struck that note when he threw a lance into the Heart of Christ and the last drop of Blood and water flowed freely. It was finished—He could give no more.

SENSITIVE

When we hear the word "sensitive" we usually think of someone who overreacts to slight offenses, or whose imagination runs away at the least provocation. This type of person is not really sensitive; he is more self-conscious, self-centered, and introverted.

Jesus, however, was sensitive in the best sense of the word. He felt the slights of other men. He felt their jealousy, ingratitude, and hatred. The difference in the sensitivity of Jesus and our own is that He never turned inward when He was hurt. He immediately realized that those who disbelieved Him were in reality offending the Father who sent Him.

When men were ungrateful, He thought of their souls, not His feelings. When they tried to trick Him, He thought of their hypocrisy and their warped spirits. He felt all the emotions that rise up in a soul from the indifference and weaknesses of other men, but He used them all as part of our Redemption. He was never weighed down by them.

One day Jesus was invited to the home of a leading Pharisee. A woman who was a sinner came in and knelt behind Jesus as He was at table. She wept and as she did so her tears fell on His feet and she wiped them with her hair (Lk. 7:36-50).

Though no one spoke a word, many at table began to criticize her in their hearts. Jesus looked at His host and said, "Simon, do you see this woman? I came into your house and you poured no water over My feet; . . . you gave Me no kiss . . . you did not anoint My head with oil."

Jesus was sensitive to every breach of etiquette that His host had perpetrated against Him. He felt every insult, and had pity on the host who obviously felt little need for His God's forgiveness or love.

On another occasion He looked over Jerusalem with its beautiful Temple and buildings and said, "Jerusalem, Jerusalem . . . How often have I longed to gather your children, as a hen gathers her chicks under her wings, and you refused" (Mt. 23:37).

His sensitive Heart wanted to reach out and embrace His children, but they were too busy. He was not the kind of Messiah they expected or desired. He felt the pangs of rejection and indifference and He looked over the city with a sad Heart.

He went to the synagogue to teach on the Sabbath and those who listened to Him were there merely to test Him. They saw a man there who had a withered hand and they wondered if Jesus would heal him.

It was a heart-rending experience to speak to a crowd knowing their thoughts were critical. Realizing His words were falling on deaf ears, Jesus looked at the afflicted man and said, "Stand up out in the middle" (Mk. 3:3).

These men were not the least bit interested in hearing the word of God or receiving light about the Messiah. They were interested only in the theological question of whether it was lawful to cure on the Sabbath.

Jesus had to force the issue and their hypocrisy out into the open. "Is it against the Law on the sabbath day to do good, or to do evil; to save life, or to kill?" They could not answer. "Then, grieved to find them so obstinate, He looked angrily round at them, and said to the man, 'Stretch out your hand', and instantly he was healed" (Mk. 3:4-5).

This miracle only antagonized the Pharisees, for they left the Temple and began to plot against Him (Mk. 3:6). Jesus tried so hard to prove His Divinity, to show the Father's love, to offer forgiveness, but there were times when all these overtures were ignored or repulsed, and His love found no response.

His Heart was saddened one day when, after He cured lepers, and cast out demons, the Scribes told Him it was through Beelzebul He cast out demons. Jesus gently asked them the question, "How can Satan cast out Satan?" (Mk. 3:23).

Jesus warned them that to have such thoughts was to sin against the Holy Spirit. To dare ascribe to Satan the signs that were wrought by the power of God in His Son was to commit the unforgivable sin. The sin was unforgivable because they had rejected God. They sought to kill Him for He was a threat to their positions. Like their father, the Devil, they would be His enemies eternally.

Though it was difficult for Jesus to be misunderstood by His enemies, it was certainly more frustrating not to be understood by His friends.

After hearing the revelation of a mystery by the use of a parable, His Apostles would ask for an explanation. They had been with Him so long; He had spoken to them in private for hours at a time and still, they did not comprehend the simplest parables.

"Do you not understand, either?" He would ask them (Mk. 7:18). Was there no one who believed what He said just because

He said it? In spite of it all, He continued to work signs and miracles. He continued to preach the Good News in simple language so everyone would understand.

However, in spite of His persevering effort, the Pharisees one day asked Him for a sign from Heaven. They were not satisfied with healings, feeding the multitudes, and casting out demons. No, it was a sign in the sky they wanted.

Scripture says, "And with a sigh that came straight from the heart, he said, 'Why does this generation demand a sign? I tell you solemnly, no sign shall be given to this generation'" (Mk. 8:12). He left them and walked away—away from their cold hearts and proud minds. He got into one of the Apostles' boats, and went to the opposite shore. It was as if He had to get away from the callous rejection of those who should have known Him, believed in Him, and loved Him.

All of His life Jesus felt the indifference, coldness, and lack of faith of His chosen people. His relatives thought He was mad and His Apostles were forever questioning His words and actions.

At the Last Supper discourse, Jesus told them that if they knew Him, they would also know the Father. He tried to explain to them that they had truly seen the Father. Jesus wanted

His followers to realize that they were to be perfect images of Him, just as He was a perfect image of the Father (Jn. 14:6-7).

As He was explaining this profound truth Philip said, "Lord, let us see the Father, and then we shall be satisfied" (Jn. 14:8).

Jesus looked at Philip as if He could not believe what He heard. "Have I been with you all this time, Philip," He replied, "and you still do not know Me? To have seen Me is to have seen the Father—so how can you say, 'Let us see the Father'?" (Jn. 14:9).

There were times it all seemed hopeless. They did not understand simple parables; they believed He was God yet were content with only His Humanity, never fully realizing His Divinity.

Jesus realized He would have to accept their dull minds and weak faith. He would send them His Spirit and then they would have the necessary light to proclaim Him Lord and King. During His lifetime, however, He would have to repeat His parables, explain His words, anticipate their questions, and manifest His Divinity.

He was happy for their love and devotion, but their incredulity and lack of comprehension would be part of His daily Cross—the Cross that would redeem them and the world.

HUMOROUS INSIGHT

It is hardly reasonable to think that the God who created man to laugh never laughed Himself. Although there is no specific passage in Scripture that indicates Jesus laughed, there are numerous passages that indicate He certainly caused other people to laugh. At least, they displayed one of those satisfying smiles one sees when a word or gesture expresses something that has long gone unsaid.

We can well imagine the men going home at night and telling their wives, "You should have heard what He said to the Pharisees today! The Master has great wit for He confounds His enemies with their own words."

One such occasion was a day the Pharisees chose to make Jesus guilty of a state crime. "Is it permissible," they asked Him, "to pay taxes to Caesar or not? Should we pay—yes or no?" "Hand Me a denarius, and let Me see it," Jesus replied. Looking at the coin, and then at the Pharisees, He said, "Whose head is this? Whose name?" "Caesar's," they told Him. "Give back to Caesar what belongs to Caesar — and to God what belongs to God" (Mk. 12:13-17).

When we read this account, we feel almost impelled to cheer and say "Bravo." Looking at this scene brings to mind another occasion when, after performing many miracles and expelling the money-changers from the Temple, He was asked by the elders, "What authority have you for acting like this?" (Mt. 21:23).

"And I," Jesus replied, "will ask you a question, only one; if you tell Me the answer to it, I will then tell you My authority for acting like this. John's Baptism: where did it come from: Heaven or man?" (Mt. 21:24-25).

The smiles on the faces of the crowd must have been broad as they all waited for the answer. If the priests and elders answered "from Heaven" Jesus would ask them why they refused to believe John. If they answered "from man," the people would rise up in anger, for they recognized John as a Prophet of the Lord.

Realizing they fell into their own trap, they answered Jesus, "We do not know." And He retorted, "Nor will I tell you My authority for acting like this" (Mt. 21:27).

It is not difficult to visualize the joy of the crowds as Jesus once more confounded His enemies and gave the people a sense of security, as they realized the Master they followed knew what He was about.

These tricky questions that related to politics were soon replaced by theological ones. If they could not antagonize the Government against Him, they would present difficult questions of Law and Morals, and thereby change public opinion.

Character assassination always begins with replacing high opinions with lower ones: first, by subtle innuendoes, then by the undermining of confidence, and finally outright lies or exaggerations.

The Pharisees' next maneuver was to find someone leading an immoral life and present the case before Jesus. The day a woman was caught in adultery seemed to the Pharisees the ideal moral question with which to trick Him (Jn. 8:1-11).

They brought her to Him, and said, "Master, this woman was caught in the very act of committing adultery, and Moses has ordered us in the Law to condemn women like this to death by stoning. What have You to say?"

It was another one of those calculated questions, designed to trap the one who answered into error, no matter what he replied. Jesus bent down and started writing on the ground with His finger.

What was Jesus writing in the sand? Was it the sins of His questioners or was He doodling as men do when they think?

After they persisted with their question, He looked up and said, "If there is one of you who has not sinned, let him be the first to throw a stone at her."

The crowd was curious as the Pharisees began to walk away "one by one, beginning with the eldest."

There were certainly many smiles among the people for they knew the evil in the lives of those who condemned this woman.

The crowd realized Jesus was not condoning the woman's sin. He looked up and said, "Woman, where are they? Has no-one condemned you?" "No-one, Sir," she replied. "Neither do I condemn you; go away, and don't sin any more."

Jesus was aware of the jealousy of the Pharisees. One day, when some of them told Him to go away from Jerusalem because Herod meant to kill Him, He said, "You may go and give that fox this message: 'Learn that today and tomorrow I cast out devils and on the third day attain My end'" (Lk. 13:32).

It is sad to see mere creatures plotting against their Creator but glorious to see that Creator defending Himself with the "flavor of wit." Even when they accused Him of casting out demons by Beelzebul, His reply was one seasoned with wry humor. "If it is through Beelzebul I cast out demons, through whom do your own experts cast them out?" (Luke 11:19).

There is one scene in the Gospels that shows the beautiful humanity of Jesus perhaps more than others. Jesus sat down by a well and was approached by a Samaritan woman (Jn. 4:1-42). This scene manifests His fatigue, His humor, His compassion, His zeal for souls, His Mercy, and His Love. Though the conversation recorded was rather serious, Jesus introduced a little humor when He asked the woman to go and call her husband. "I have no husband," she answered.

Jesus certainly nodded with a smile on His face when He replied, "You are right to say, 'I have no husband' for, although you have had five, the one you have now is not your husband."

Though many contend Jesus never laughed, it is impossible to have joy and not exhibit those facial expressions that depict this God-given emotion.

The seventy-two disciples went to Jesus rejoicing that even the demons were subject to them and Scripture records Jesus' reaction to their exuberance. "It was then that, filled with joy by the Holy Spirit, He said, 'I bless You, Father, Lord of Heaven and earth, for hiding these things from the learned and the clever and revealing them to mere children'" (Lk. 10:21). His joy was evident to everyone, and it is this joy that He promised would be ours — the joy that comes from the Holy Spirit.

"Later, while teaching in the Temple, Jesus said, 'How can the Scribes maintain that the Christ is the son of David?... David himself calls Him Lord, in what way then can He be his son?' And the great majority of the people heard this with delight" (Mark 12:35, 37). The Pharisees admitted that the Messiah would be the son of David, for David referred to Him as "Lord."

Jesus was so insistent about His disciples being full of joy that He exhorted them to wash their faces and anoint their hands when they fasted so no one would see their sacrifice except the Father in Heaven (Mt. 6:16-18).

They were not to pull gloomy faces like the Pharisees but they were to radiate the joy and peace of the Holy Spirit.

In the Old Testament, we find two unusual passages. "He (God) hoists a signal for a distant nation, he whistles it up from the ends of the earth" (Is. 5:26). And "I am going to whistle to them and gather them in (for I will redeem them)" (Zech. 10:8).

Humorous Insight

The Son, whose Father inspired holy men to picture Him whistling the nations together, smiled and was full of joy, for He is Infinite Love, and Love produces laughter.

JESUS, OUR MODEL

Jesus showed us how to act and react under every circumstance. He loved us so much that He wanted to experience all the pain, joy, suffering, weakness, and the consequences of our fallen nature.

Though He was without sin, He took upon Himself our frailties and by so doing raised us up to a higher level.

Because He experienced everything we are (sin excepted), He desired that we experience everything He is.

He merited for each of us a Divine Participation in His very Nature. Through the Power of His Spirit, who pours grace into our souls, we are now sons of God and heirs to the Kingdom.

As heirs, we must resemble the Father whose children we are. As sons, we must resemble the Son whose brothers we are. As Participators, we must resemble the Spirit whose Power makes us the Beloved of Infinite Love.

His love made Him want to be like us and our love must make us want to be like Him.

Our individual personalities must be enhanced by those parallel qualities in Jesus. If we are kind by nature, then that kindness must take on Divine Kindness by Grace, which goes beyond our natural capabilities.

Those qualities of soul that do not resemble Jesus must be changed and transformed into Him. We shall all resemble Him in different ways and this variety will glorify the Father and be an unending source of joy for all eternity.

The Christian's goal in life is to be a perfect image of Jesus, as Jesus is the perfect image of the Father. The beloved features of the Master are ever imprinted upon the Christian's mind. The words of the Master burn in his heart as they did in the hearts of the disciples going to Emmaus. The Christian reaches up to his Savior in an increasing act of prayerful thanksgiving for his redemption and sonship.

He looks at Jesus in His strength and tries to be strong.

He sees Jesus gentle to the crowds and he controls his anger.

He admires the Mercy of Jesus and he forgives seventy times seven.

He feels the Compassion of Jesus and he becomes sensitive to the needs of others.

He is humbled by the humility of Jesus and he conquers his pride.

He sees Jesus heroic, courageous, and unafraid and he is assured.

He watches Jesus as He answers His enemies in a serene tone of voice — truthful, without human respect, with perfect self-control — and he tries to be like Him.

He imitates the Master's sense of loyalty, zeal, simplicity, nobility, and loving qualities to the best of his ability. This becomes a way of life for a Christian, for he is not satisfied with giving his God thanksgiving, he desires to give Him perfect praise by imitation.

Most of all, he imitates the Master's way of loving — without counting the cost — even unto death.

"And we, with our unveiled faces reflecting like mirrors the brightness of the Lord, all grow brighter and brighter as we are turned into the Image that we reflect" (2 Cor. 3:18).

THE FRUITS
OF HIS LOVE

THE NEW FRUIT

Jesus has asked me to bear fruit—fruit that will last—and when I do, I will glorify the Father.

The modern age in which I live, with its high standard of living and materialistic culture, demands virtues never thought of before.

To bring me up to modern demands, the Sanctifier seems to be giving different lights on various qualities of soul that must be raised to a higher plane.

In the past I was called upon to be sympathetic, which gave me a feeling of sorrow for the pain and disappointments of my neighbor.

Today I am expected to have empathy—that disposition by which I put myself in another person's shoes, feel what he feels, understand his actions and judge with more compassion.

In the past I was expected to lend an ear to a neighbor's problems or opinions, and it was enough to be attentive.

Today I am expected to listen with loving attention, be willing to learn, be humble enough to change if necessary, and be totally interested in all he has to say. I am asked to be Objective.

In the past I was virtuous when I was tolerant—meaning I endured anyone different than myself.

Today I am asked to be receptive to everyone and to regard only those things that unite us rather than the things that separate us.

In the past I was asked to be generous, which meant an unselfish giving.

Today I am expected to be magnanimous and to give my love, my talents, my time, and my possessions to God and my neighbor.

In the past, anyone dedicated to God's service played the part of doctor, lawyer, counselor, interpreter, and judge.

Today, an educated minister of God is only one among a congregation of educators and educated. He is not expected to compete with the intellectuals in his flock but to be holy with the holiness of God—perfect, always available, discerning, and compassionate.

All the qualities and dispositions of soul that I was called upon to manifest to my neighbor in the past were good and satisfying. But today, God demands more, because more is needed and He desires me to reach for the heights.

I must not look into the past and see what others have accomplished. I must be the kind of Christian the Spirit desires me to be — in this time in history, in this place, in this state of life, and with my temperament.

These and many other qualities are signs of a Christian. The purpose of a sign is to give information, direction, witness to a truth, and show power. My life must bear many of these signs if I am to bear fruit and glorify the Father.

My neighbor should be able to read these signs readily and be inspired to follow where they lead.

Some signs I already possess, for they form part of my temperament. Others I must acquire through His grace and my effort.

Some will come rather easily, and others will take time, patience, and suffering to acquire.

Some I will possess in a high degree and others I may hardly manifest.

Only Jesus had the fullness of these qualities, and He gave them to His Mother Mary, the Apostles, and all the People of God, in varying degrees throughout the centuries.

His Will, His mission for me, my temperament, the culture in which I live, etc., will all pull together to build up these qualities in my soul. In every situation — be it joy, when I bear the fruit of gratitude, or sorrow, when I bear the fruit of patience — the image of Jesus will become brighter and brighter.

I can be sure of one thing: regardless of my state in life, I am called by God to be holy with a holiness that comes from Him but is uniquely mine.

I must aspire to be the kind of saint He desires me to be, and bear the kind of fruit that will express His designs in my soul in time and in eternity.

Every moment of time plants a seed that bears fruit — fruit that will form a part of my happiness for all eternity.

The seeds of pain bear the fruit of patience; disappointment bears the fruit of resignation; joy bears the fruit of gratitude; success bears the fruit of praise; and all of them, as they imprint His Image on my soul, enhance my glory for all eternity.

I must water these seeds as they are planted by the Divine Gardener so they may grow strong and bear much fruit.

Fruits of His Love

There are times in my daily life when I need to fan into a flame, as St. Paul told Timothy, the Gifts that have been given to me (2 Tim. 1:6).

I must look at every moment of life as an opportunity to be more like Jesus. I am called upon by God and neighbor to manifest kindness, mercy, love, and many other qualities of soul.

Jesus promised that with Him in me I would bear much fruit, but alone, I would not be able to do anything (Jn. 15:5).

The Seven Gifts given to me at Baptism, along with Faith, Hope, and Love, all work together to bring out of my soul those beautiful qualities that are hidden and covered by the weakness of my nature.

The Gifts uncover these qualities and I become more and more like Jesus. This growing in the Lord gives my neighbor courage for his own trials, and gives me more joy and peace.

It is a mystery difficult to comprehend. It is Jesus in me who bears the fruit—and yet, I am the one who manifests the fruit.

His Power, His Grace, and His Gifts in me must be manifest to my neighbor. I must render to my neighbor those things I cannot render to God, and God in His Infinite Goodness counts it as done to Himself.

This twofold combination—His Grace and my will—must work together in perfect harmony if the fruit is to be beautiful and plentiful.

There is a scene in the Resurrection narratives that might explain this combined Power:

The Apostles had labored all night on the Sea of Tiberius and had caught nothing. They were about to come in when they saw a lone figure on the shore. A voice cried out, "Have you caught anything, friends?" And when they answered "No," He said "Throw the net out to starboard and you'll find something." So they dropped the net and there were so many fish they could not haul it in (Jn. 21:4-6).

The Apostles had labored all night; they were discouraged, frustrated, and tired. A stranger on the shore makes a rather ridiculous request, asking them to throw the net on the starboard side to find a catch.

The important point here is that the Apostles did what they were requested to do, and they portrayed three qualities of soul: obedience, faith, and motivated effort.

They did not argue with the stranger — they threw over the net immediately and this showed their desire for a catch and their faith that perhaps — there was a chance. Even though the chance of a catch of fish at dawn was slim, they would take it.

The net became heavy with fish almost immediately and they realized the stranger was the Lord.

As they drew into shore, the Master made another request. He asked them to bring in some of the fish *they* had caught (Jn. 21:10).

This is a strange request. He told them where and when to throw the net; He filled it with fish; yet He says it was all *their* catch.

Perhaps this is an example of the harmony that must exist between His Grace and my will.

I must have great desires, the Faith to realize His Word is true, and the effort to accomplish what His Will requests of me.

I will look at these three qualities — obedience, faith, and effort — and see how they are of benefit in my daily life.

OBEDIENCE

I must not look upon obedience as an unbearable yoke that chokes my freedom.

I must see it as He saw it — a great means of strengthening my will and freeing me from the slavery of my unbridled emotions.

Obedience manifests a preferential love, meaning that I prefer God's Will to my own, as manifested to me by the civil authorities, religious authority, parents, the needs of my neighbor, and my obligations to God.

Obedience adds a strong dimension to my life: it means I *will* to obey, and I obey out of love — love for God, neighbor, and myself.

It may be difficult but that only makes it more meritorious and more loving. It certainly takes more love to obey when it is difficult than when it is easy.

There is a definite, positive aspect of obedience that I may miss completely. It molds me into the image of Jesus in a special way. He was obedient unto death, and His humility in submitting to His own creatures redeemed me from the slavery of sin.

Obedience is a strong virtue, capable of making me master of my emotions by giving me more strength to conquer my pride as I submit to those above me out of respect for their God-given authority, and to those below me out of love.

Jesus reminded Pilate that he would have no authority over Him if it were not given to him from above. I must remember this when obeying is painful: it is the Lord I obey. I must realize that if I ever reach the attitude that no one can tell me what to do, then I am being guided by a fool. I will be tossed back and forth by the waves of dissention and crushed against the rocks of bitterness. I will finally find myself a loner on the shore of life, never understanding where I went wrong.

The Father uses obedience to chip away the disfigurations that pride has caused in my soul, to strengthen my will, to quiet my doubts when I wonder what to do, and to raise me above myself so I can resemble His Son

Scripture

You who wanted no sacrifice or obligation, prepared a body for me. You took no pleasure in holocausts or sacrifices for sin; then I said, just as I was commanded in the scroll of the book, "God, here I am! I am coming to obey Your Will." (Heb. 10:5-7)

Obey your leaders and do as they tell you, because they must give an account of the way they look after your souls; make this a joy for them to do, and not a grief—you yourselves would be the losers. (Heb. 13:17)

FAITH

When speaking of Faith, I often think of it as relating only to God. But what about Faith in my neighbor? The Apostles portrayed a deep faith in their neighbor as they obeyed the request to throw over the net for a catch. They did not know at that time it was the Lord — it was only a stranger who called them "Friends."

Considering the traumatic experience the Apostles recently had as the people vented their anger and hatred on their Lord at the crucifixion, it is remarkable that these men of God retained any faith in their fellow-man, at least the kind of faith it must have taken to comply with the request of a stranger.

They did not permit the weakness of some men to warp their faith in other men.

I must not permit the evil capabilities of human nature to sour my faith in the tremendous good that is possible, despite the frailty of that nature. A friend may fail often and disappoint me, but I cannot lose faith in him.

Jesus did not lose faith in Peter despite his threefold denial. He gave him the keys of the Kingdom as He promised, realizing that Peter's fall would be the foundation of his humility, and, rooted in this virtue, he would stand firm to the end.

My brother may offend me seventy times seven but my faith in him should rise to the occasion, give him the benefit of the doubt, and forgive him. His knowledge that his offenses have not lessened my faith in his inner goodness will help him gain confidence in himself.

Most people try hard to please, and my faith in them must be strong enough to ride the tide of failure as they voyage home.

Even if my fellow-man has proven faithless time after time, I can at least retain a hope that he will improve, pray for him, and think kindly, without frustration and disappointment.

Jesus gave me a beautiful example of an undying faith in my neighbor by the way He treated Judas. To the very last, at the moment he betrayed Him, Jesus called him "Friend."

My faith may not go that far but at least I can try to build rather than destroy, to overcome rather than to succumb, to be confident rather than doubtful, and raise sullen spirits with a friendly, "You can do it."

Scripture

Question your friend, he may have done nothing at all, and if he has done anything, he will not do it again.

Question your neighbor, he may have said nothing at all, and if he has said anything, he will not say it again.

Question your friend, for slander is very common; do not believe all you hear.

A man sometimes makes a slip, without meaning what he says; and which of us has never sinned by speech?

Question your neighbor before you threaten him and leave scope for the Law of the Most High. (Sir. 19:13-17)

MOTIVATED EFFORT

If the Apostles had analyzed the stranger's request, they would never have complied with it. Every fisherman knows you do not throw a net over the starboard side of a boat, and common sense would have told them that if they had not made a catch all night they would surely not make one at dawn.

But they did not stop to look at the obstacles; they wanted only one thing—a catch of fish. Behind the effort of throwing over the net was a motive—a motive strong enough to overcome the impossible.

I must be sure that behind all my actions there is a motive. The effort I put forth in accomplishing the smallest task must have some motive behind it.

An action without a motive is like a boat without a rudder. It sails aimlessly across the sea of life, pushed to and fro by the wind of futility.

The prime motive behind every work must be the love of God, and secondly, the good of my neighbor. Selfish motives may give my actions more thrust for the moment, but in the end I will find them empty and turned into ashes.

My Effort will never arrive at its highest peak of performance unless it has not only motivation, but enthusiasm.

There is a tendency to work and accomplish the tasks of daily living with a "forced labor" attitude.

I *must* work to eat, I *must* be nice or people will not like me, I *must* go to church because it is expected of me, I *must* obey or I get into trouble, I *must* go to college because everyone goes these days, I *must* make money because I'll be respected for it — these and many more shallow motives drain my soul of that bubbling and long-lasting enthusiasm that accompanies a task done for the love of God rather than myself.

This enthusiasm is not based on the successful outcome of my efforts. Its roots are in God, and in the realization that I have made an effort to be good and do good. If failure is the result, I must understand that God accepts my efforts.

My failures may be my greatest successes. It is in failure that I have often drawn closer to God, learned to depend more on

Him than myself, gained self-knowledge, and seen things in their right perspective.

If I continue to learn these lasting lessons from disappointment and failure, I can afford to continue being enthusiastic about the future and my capabilities.

There is another aspect of enthusiasm that I must not overlook. It is the enthusiasm of other people.

When I observe my neighbor joyously enthused about anything, I must be careful not to put a damper on his joy. The object of his happiness may not affect me personally, but if it affects him and increases his well-being, I must be receptive to his enthusiasm out of love rather than personal interest.

Prayer

O God, let me maintain my faith in my neighbor's inner goodness, despite his many failings. Let all my efforts, in both material and spiritual areas, be motivated by the highest principles and mixed with an unfailing enthusiasm.

Scripture

All the runners at the stadium are trying to win, but only one of them gets the prize. You must run in the same way, meaning to win. All the fighters at the games go into strict training; they do this just to win a wreath that will wither away, but we do it for a wreath that will never wither. That is how I run, intent on winning; that is how I fight, not beating the air. (1 Cor. 9:24-26)

HUMBLE SERVICE

Jesus asked His Apostles one day if they thought a master was obliged to thank his servant for serving him a meal before the servant had his own meal. The answer was an obvious "No." He then proceeded to say, "So with you; when you have done all you have been told to do, say, 'We are merely servants; we have done no more than our duty'" (Luke 17:7-10).

Humility is difficult in everyday life and is often mistaken for weakness. But it is far from that. Humility is ...

- the strength to face up to myself without discouragement,
- the ability to compare myself with God and rejoice in His Greatness,
- to rejoice when I manage an unselfish deed and give the credit to Him,
- the desire to serve when His Providence places me in a position of authority,

- to rise after a fall with repentant love rather than despairing pity,
- to be of real service to those in need without a feeling of condescension,
- the ability to wait my turn to speak during a heated discussion,
- to be at peace when others surpass me in talents and accomplishments, realizing that all good things come from God,
- to listen with a spirit of objectivity rather than an 'I know it all' attitude,
- to be content with what I am but confident that His grace can make me better,
- to be obedient to those in authority without resentment,
- to be available to everyone at all times, knowing He will make up for what I lack,
- the desire to please rather than be pleased,
- and most of all, to believe His revelations, hope in His Word, and love Him more than myself.

It takes great strength to be humble because I must accept myself as I am, accept others as they are, and be neither discouraged nor surprised at human frailty. That is to be strong!

Humility prevents me from taking things personally, and this frees me from misunderstandings and heartaches. Humility is truth, and the truth is, that although I can do nothing, He can do everything in me, and this keeps me from feeling inferior. This truth really makes me free.

Being humble also frees me from those feelings of injustice that sometimes plague my soul. It is more important what God thinks than what man thinks, for God judges my interior and man judges my exterior.

Only God sees both, for He knows my sorrow after a fall, my cry for help in times of distress, my prayer in pain, my tears when I'm alone, my loneliness in a crowded street, and my love in times of dryness.

My neighbor can judge only from what he sees and that is only part of me. I must not be harsh then, when his judgment is wrong. I must remember this and be humble when I am misjudged and be content that God understands.

Humility doesn't mean I make myself a doormat for everyone to walk on. Jesus was humble and that very humility gave Him the courage to tell the Pharisees they were full of dead men's bones (Mt. 23:27). His humility kept him from human respect and made Him more interested in how their hatred was warping their own souls than how it affected His image in the eyes of the people.

His humility also gave him perseverance in doing good in the face of the ingratitude of the nine lepers and many others who sought after him for selfish motives (Lk. 17:17-18). Humility is self-effacing and perhaps that is what often makes it repugnant. But self-effacement is not belittling or annihilating. It does not destroy.

It is very positive — it merely removes those qualities in me that are not like Jesus and makes room for those dispositions of soul that elevate me above myself.

The Master said many times that unless a grain of wheat falls into the ground and dies it will remain alone (Jn. 12:24).

Self-effacement, whose fruit is humility, does just that — it aids me in getting rid of selfishness, self-interest, and inordinate self-love. It frees my mind from a constant preoccupation with self, and leaves my soul open in order to be filled with God.

Humility is that quality most pleasing to God because it faces truth with love and peace. The truth being in this case that everything I am and have comes from God, and I look to Him alone for a constant influx of goodness and love.

It makes me prefer to be of service rather than be served, and to be good rather than be the recipient of goodness.

I must know my place before God and be content with my place before men. If I am not as high in the estimation of others as I think I deserve, then let me think of Jesus who was accounted as a "Nobody." He was content, for many years, that the Father and Mary alone knew His true greatness.

True greatness is to reflect Jesus to my neighbor. My ambition then is for the spiritual gifts. But these things need the deep roots of humility in order to grow and bear fruit.

Jesus in His Goodness wants me to share in everything He does for me. I must keep in mind that He has endowed me with intelligence, physical strength, talents, friends, and everything else that contributes to my good.

My sharing consists in using them. He and I work together towards holiness in the spiritual life and success in the material world.

He wants me to feel I have done something, but He does not want me to forget the source of all the good things I possess.

When I take all the credit for my accomplishments, it is a lie — it is pride.

As humility is truth — Pride is falsehood.

The real truth then is that He and I work together — every minute — in everything. I can do nothing alone; therefore, it is wrong to take the *entire* credit for my talents and accomplishments.

Our working harmoniously together bears much fruit. That is why Jesus could tell His disciples at the Sea of Tiberius to bring in some of the fish *they* had caught even though He directed them and filled the net.

The Apostles were discouraged and knew it was nothing they had done to obtain such a catch, but Jesus didn't want them to be disheartened — only humble.

So He gave them the opportunity to use their talents and effort to bring in what His Goodness gave them.

They worked together. That catch was the Lord's and theirs, and they were content to state the truth for all men to read. That is humility.

Scripture

My son, be gentle in carrying out your business, and you will be better loved than a lavish giver. The greater you are, the more you should behave humbly, and then you will find favor with the Lord; for great though the power of the Lord is, He accepts the homage of the humble. (Sir. 3:17-19)

At this time the disciples came to Jesus and said, "Who is the greatest in the kingdom of heaven?" So He called a little child to Him and set the child in front of them. Then He said, "I tell you solemnly, unless you change and become like little children you will never enter the kingdom of heaven. And so, the one who makes himself as this little child is the greatest in the kingdom of heaven. (Mt. 18:1-4)

Shoulder my yoke and learn from Me, for I am gentle and humble in heart, and you will find rest for your souls. (Mt. 11:29)

There must be no competition among you, no conceit, but everybody is to be self-effacing. Always consider the other person to be better than yourself, so that nobody thinks of his own interests first, but everybody thinks of other people's interests instead. In your minds you must be the same as Christ Jesus.

His state was divine, yet He did not cling to His equality with God, but emptied Himself to assume the condition of a slave.... He was humbler yet, even to accepting death, death on a Cross. (Phil. 2:3-7, 8)

Prayer

Lord God, give me the grace to be humble, self-effacing, and gentle in my dealings with my neighbor. Empty me of me that I may be filled with thee.

RESPONSIBLE DETACHMENT

One day Jesus told His disciples to be careful about money because it is capable of possessing our souls, and yet, God blessed Solomon with great riches.

The disciples themselves had a purse from which they drew for everyday expenses.

The question then is not whether or not you have money or don't have money, the real question is whether you possess money or money possesses you!

As long as the world exists, there will be rich and poor, and both states of life have their advantages and disadvantages.

A rich man can be poor in spirit, compassionate, generous, and seek the one thing necessary in life — God's Will and Love.

But if his riches become his god, then money is an evil. He no longer thanks God for his success, or uses his surplus for the good of others; it is his — all his.

Although he may have an accumulation of this world's goods, he is in reality the poorest of the poor. He has sold all he has to buy land but has lost the pearl of great price (Mt. 13:45-46).

A poor man may have little, but if he possesses faith and trust he can survive on that little and be free to love God and his neighbor and enjoy all the things God has given him in nature, in his family, and in the world. He has no one to envy him, persecute him, or covet his goods. He is free to concentrate on the spiritual riches that last. Those riches he can possess in abundance.

But if a poor man is hateful of those who have more than he, or wishes in his heart only one thing—money—if this occupies his mind, makes him bitter and pretentious, then he is rich in his heart and destitute in reality.

As I contemplate these possibilities, I realize that neither riches nor poverty are in themselves of any consequence.

My heart will be where my treasure is, and that must be in God. Rich or poor, I must have a responsible detachment, and know that whether I possess great riches or give all to the poor, without God and His Love it would be nothing.

My love for God and my compassion for my neighbor must not be measured by worldly possessions, meaning I love God only when I have all my desires fulfilled.

Neither is my compassion and kindness measured by a feeling of superiority when I possess more than others.

Material possessions or the lack of these possessions must remain outside of me and never interfere with my life with God or the good I accomplish.

My goodness must have its source in Him, and the radiance of that goodness is the fruit of His Love.

The Master has never asked that I make myself destitute. He never asked that I give everything and thus become a burden on society.

He desires that I work to maintain myself and my family and that I share with others when they are in need.

In speaking of money and possessions, He said, "If then you cannot be trusted with money, that tainted thing, who will trust you with genuine riches!" (Lk. 16:11).

If the worldly things that God in His Goodness gives to me, possess me, control me, and make me proud and arrogant, then how can He trust me with great gifts of soul?

If material things make me proud, limit my vision and desire for heavenly treasures, then how can He bestow spiritual graces upon me?

If I fall beneath the weight of a splinter, how can I carry a beam?

If I am satisfied with only the things I can see, feel, hear, and touch, then how can He give me the vision to see the unseen?

If I desire to serve only those who promote my glory, pride, ambition, and comfort, then how will I ever wait upon the humble, self-effacing, and unpretentious Christ?

Truly, if Jesus cannot trust me to use material possessions to further His Kingdom, then He will be unable to trust me with those powerful spiritual possessions that must be used with prudence, humility, and love.

Prayer

Lord and Father, I desire to use the things of this world for Thy honor and glory. Give me the grace to be faithful in little things that I may be trusted with great things.

Scripture

A man labors and toils and forges ahead only to find himself the more out-distanced. Another man is a poor creature begging for assistance, badly off for support, but rich in poverty, and the Lord turns a favorable eye on him, sets him on his feet out of his abject condition, and enables him to hold his head high, to the utter amazement of many.

Good and bad, life and death, poverty and wealth, all come from the Lord. (Sir. 11:11-14)

Do not give your heart to your money, or say, "With this I am self-sufficient.... Who has authority over me?... I have sinned and what happened to me?... His compassion is great, He will forgive my many sins."

Do not be so sure of forgiveness that you add sin to sin.

Do not set your heart on ill-gotten gains; they will be of no use to you on the day of disaster. (Sir. 5:1, 3, 4, 6, 5, 8)

FORGIVENESS AND MERCY

In the Gospel of St. Luke, Jesus tells me that if my brother offends me seven times a day, and seven times comes to me and says he is sorry, then I must forgive him (Luke 17:4).

But in the Gospel of St. Matthew, when Peter asked Jesus if he should forgive his brother seven times when he was offended, the Master answered, "Not seven times, but seventy times seven" (Mt. 18:22).

The first counsel in Luke demands forgiveness as often as forgiveness is asked. The second brings me up to a higher plane and requires me to have mercy of heart even when forgiveness is not asked.

In the Lord's prayer that Jesus gave me, He requests that I be forgiven by God in the same way I forgive my brother.

It seems then that the matter of forgiveness is clear; God expects me to forgive in my words, in my heart, and in my deeds.

In My Words

When I see my brother has acquired a sinful habit, Jesus said I must reprove him and if he is sorry and says so, I must forgive.

There are times when a neighbor may offend me and not know it.

I must have the courage to bring this to his attention, not so much because of the offense done to me but because this fault in him may offend God and make him unChristlike.

When he says he is sorry, I must be very quick to forgive and do so as often as he says he is sorry.

It takes humility to ask forgiveness and I cannot respond with pride by not forgiving.

Humility is the requisite for both asking forgiveness, and accepting repentance.

This is where I need empathy and self-knowledge.

I must put myself in my neighbor's shoes, take upon myself his personality, understand his dispositions, and know that I would be capable of the same fault were I in his place.

I am very quick to forgive and excuse myself because I know the motives for my actions. Since I do not know my brother's interior dispositions, I must give him the benefit of the doubt in the same way as I do myself.

Even though I may not be as weak as my brother is in many areas, I must remember I also have my faults and he, too, must forgive me many times.

Since asking forgiveness is a requisite for being forgiven, I must be ready to say I am sorry when I offend my brother.

The account in St. Luke requires that I gently correct, forgive when asked, and seek forgiveness myself by an acknowledgement of my offenses.

When my neighbor refuses to admit an offense or ask forgiveness, then I must have recourse to the next counsel and develop the disposition of . . .

Mercy of the Heart

As Jesus hung on the Cross, He asked His Father to forgive His enemies because they did not know what they were doing.

They had not asked forgiveness and neither were many of them conscious they had done anything wrong. The people were deluded by the priests and Pharisees, and the soldiers were following the orders of Pilate. The centurion was enlightened only after he pierced Jesus' side.

Although Jesus suffered intensely, many of those responsible were sincere and thought they were doing a service to God.

Jesus could and did ask forgiveness for them even though He suffered at their hands.

His forgiveness was from His Heart, prompted by love, mercy, and understanding.

I may not be called upon to exercise mercy in that degree, but there are many times in my life when I can forgive and forget because my offenders have no idea of the cross they have placed on my shoulders.

A brother must be forgiven and treated as a friend because he has given me the opportunity to be like my Father in Heaven who lets His sun rise and shine on the just and the unjust.

God has used my brother's frailties to give me the opportunity to be like Jesus—merciful and forgiving.

It does not always follow that my brother and I will ever be bosom friends. But it does mean I wish him well, pray for him, and hold no grudge or resentment.

Sometimes personalities clash, and all the good will I can muster does not change the situation. Here I need to pray for the Gift of Counsel to discern the course I should take, and for mercy that I may lovingly forgive.

Then it is that I will have that disposition of soul so necessary to say the Lord's prayer with sincerity and portray ...

Forgiveness by My Deeds

It is difficult after forgiving an injury to forget the incident entirely, and yet, this is exactly the kind of forgiveness I expect and hope for from God.

I want my faults and sins to be erased from the Book of Life, and I rely on His Mercy to do so.

He will do exactly that, but He asks in return that I do the same to my brother.

He gave me the parable about the man whose master forgave him a debt of nine million dollars, and who in turn would not forgive a fellow servant a debt of less than fifteen dollars (Mat. 18:23-35).

I must keep this in mind when my brother offends me—a finite, sinful creature—and when I offend God—Infinite and All-Holy.

This does not mean my brother has a right to offend me, but it does mean that I must not exaggerate that offense out of proportion, be unforgiving and never forget.

I may be deeply hurt and my brother unjust, but I am only asked by God to forgive as He forgives me.

As with love, so with mercy; I am able to render to my neighbor what I cannot render to God—mercy and forgiveness.

When God forgives me He always gives me some token of that forgiveness. It may be a light-hearted feeling or more grace to overcome myself the next time.

His Goodness is so great and His Mercy so infinite that He rejoices over my repentance and treats me as a long-lost son.

Jesus manifested this Attribute of the Father by the parable of the Prodigal Son and said that even the Angels rejoice over my repentance (Lk. 15:11-32).

This forgiving is a trait I too must acquire. I must give my brother some sign that I rejoice in his repentance.

Perhaps a smile, a handshake are sufficient, or some token of my continued confidence in him as a person—making him realize I do not think less of him because of his offense.

I may make my brother something or purchase a gift, but if circumstances prevent me from doing this, I can at least give him the gift of my love, mercy, and kindness.

Prayer

Just and Holy God, whose mercy is higher than the heavens, grant me the grace to forgive by my words, heart, and deeds. I desire to be like Jesus and to hold no resentments or grudges. I put all my friends and enemies in Your loving hands.

Scripture

Forgive your neighbor the hurt he does you, and when you pray your sins will be forgiven. If a man nurses anger against another, can he then demand compassion from the Lord? Showing no pity for a man like himself, can he then plead for his own sins?

Mere creature of flesh, he cherishes resentment; who will forgive him his sins?

Remember the last things and stop hating, remember dissolution and death, and live by the Commandments.

Remember the Commandments, and do not bear your neighbor ill will;

Remember the Covenant of the Most High, and overlook the offense. (Sir. 28: 2-7)

POWER OF EXAMPLE

Jesus told me many times during His life to be careful that the light inside of me is not darkness. I must be careful not to light a lamp only to put it under a bushel. It must be seen by men to give them light (Lk. 11:33-36).

He also said I was not to parade my good works to be seen by men (Mt. 6:1-18).

This all seems to be a contradiction but it is not. The one applies to my interior life and the other to my exterior works.

I must not forget the power of holiness of life. If I strive for union with God, that union will manifest itself to my neighbor in many hidden ways.

Jesus described this when He said, "If, therefore, your whole body is filled with light, and no trace of darkness, it will be light entirely, as when a light shines on you with its rays" (Luke 11:36).

Those rays of God's Love shining forth from a soul united to Him, affect every person that soul meets.

The soul itself may not be conscious of its effect on others, but its example of constancy, courage, faith, and love shine out to others like the rays of the sun.

It is enough for a soul that its Lord alone knows its suffering and pain; its only desire is to witness to the joy of belonging to such a Lord.

The rays of the sun are not conscious of their varied effect on everything they touch. They are so much a part of the sun that no one notices they are only rays.

So it is with holiness of life. The soul can be so filled with God and His Love that it is not conscious of its effect on others.

As it is impossible to prevent the rays from issuing from the energy of the sun, so it is impossible to be united to God in the depths of my soul and not affect my neighbor.

Bearing the fruit of holiness proves to my neighbor that there is a God. It raises me above myself and permits me to accomplish works whose only source is God.

It gives my neighbor courage and assurance that he, too, can conquer and overcome.

Jesus often hides this type of witnessing from me to protect me from pride, but my faith assures me that my example affects the whole Mystical Body.

The more of Jesus I let shine through me, the happier will my neighbor be.

This kind of witness is powerful and safe because it is hidden. But men must also see my good works and here I often run into danger.

The Master did not say I should not perform good works. In fact, at the Last Supper discourse He said my exterior works would glorify the Father.

What the Master does not want is that I *parade* my good works. I am to do them for the love of God and neighbor and let it go at that.

To brag about them and bring them up whenever a crowd assembles, is to have my reward. The good works I do for my neighbor will be "put on." It is obvious to everyone but myself that it is all false.

My good works must spring from a deep Love for God, confidence in His power, and a real concern for my brother. Then it is that my whole life gives glory to the Father.

I can give scandal by a bad example and by no example. A lukewarm Christian can do more harm than one who is leading a sinful life.

A "do nothing" attitude can make my neighbor apathetic and hopeless. It is better for my neighbor to see me try and fail than not to try at all.

Everything I am and everything I do influences someone for better or for worse. I need not be self-conscious and think only of my example. But neither must I forget that other people are influenced by my example and that example speaks a thousand words.

Everyone is important to God and the world. A sick old woman in an apartment, unnoticed and unwanted by her neighbor, may, if she keeps close to God, help to save the very person who rejects her.

To help others enter the Kingdom, by word, work, and example, makes each person an ambassador of God, sent to heal, to console, to give hope, and to intercede on behalf of mankind.

It is not important I am seen by men, for God can use my life, example, prayers, and union with Him, to do great things—things I will know only in Eternity—but Eternity is where it counts.

Even when I am in public view, it will be the spirit with which I do things, rather than what I do, that will edify my neighbor. Better to build a house on the rock of love than a castle on the sand of selfishness. The spirit I possess will show, and the spirit either builds up or tears down.

I will make every effort to correspond to the grace He gives me that I may bear fruit to glorify the Father and encourage my neighbor.

Prayer

Lord and Father, it is Your Will that I be like Jesus. Let my life be patterned after His that I may do the works He did because You live in me.

Scripture

If you serve Christ in this way you will please God and be respected by men. So let us adopt any custom that leads to peace and our mutual improvement. (Rom. 14:18-19)

Guard against foul talk; let your words be for the improvement of others, as occasion offers, and do good to your listeners, otherwise you will only be grieving the Holy Spirit of God who has marked you with His seal for you to be set free when the day comes. (Eph. 4:29-30)

Alas for the world that there should be obstacles! Obstacles indeed there must be, but alas for the man who provides them! ... See that you never despise any one of these little ones, for I tell you that their angels in heaven are continually in the presence of My Father in heaven. (Mt. 18:7, 10)

Self-Control and Repentance

When John the Baptist went about preaching, he often said to the crowds, "If you are repentant, produce the appropriate fruit, and do not presume to tell yourselves, 'We have Abraham for our father'" (Mt. 3:8-9).

I must not think that when I have sorrow for my faults, sins, and imperfections, God is satisfied and I can go my way and do the same thing over, or that He has saved me and I can do as I please.

Although I may fall repeatedly, God judges my sincerity by the effort I put forth to overcome those things in me that are not pleasing to Him.

If I cannot bear the fruit of success, I can at least bear the fruit of effort.

My repentance must be proven by a change of life and here is where I need self-control.

Over-indulgence and a lack of self-control cause many sins. It is a lack of self-control that makes me ...

- lash out at my brother in a burst of anger,
- show impatience with my neighbor,
- talk about the faults of others,
- speak before I think,
- be intemperate in things that cause me pleasure,
- buy things I cannot afford,
- be brutally frank and caustic at times, and
- criticize the faults of others publicly.

The desire to satisfy my every whim brings upon my soul misery untold. Without self-control—that power to say NO to myself—my will is weakened and I become a slave.

Self-control will grow stronger in proportion as my repentance is sincere.

When I tell God I am sorry for having offended Him, this contrition must be followed by the determination never to commit that fault again. Repentance without a firm resolution to improve is no repentance at all.

I cannot blame people and circumstances for my offenses, though both may be involved. It is my Will that decides my actions, and a lack of control over that will is the real cause of my faults.

It often happens that I am truly sorry and resolve never to offend God again, and still I fall. No matter: if I have put forth my maximum effort, and again I am truly repentant, I can be sure my will was strengthened, though not blessed with complete success.

Discouragement weakens my self-control with an "it's no use" attitude, and this can destroy me. My progress may be slow—but it *is* progress—and slowly my self-control and repentance will be in balance and one will be as strong as the other.

Though I take three steps forward and two steps back, I have advanced one step. I must accept my slow progress as part of the penance I offer to God in reparation for my offenses.

I cannot expect to accomplish great things if I have been faithless in little things. Lack of self-control leads to spiritual weakness, and, like physical weakness, it takes time and patience to strengthen.

I need a double dose of patience and humility to accept the consequences of my faults and sins. Slowly, self-control will follow and my Will—centered more on God than on myself—will be in control of situations instead of situations being in control of me.

It is easier to control others than to control myself, but unless I do possess self-control, my control of others will be short-lived and ineffective.

I must acquire a habit of seeing God's Will and Love behind everything, and in this manner give myself some time to think before I lose control over my will and emotions.

Sometimes the realization of His Divine Presence within me and around me is a great help towards self-control.

Sometimes His suffering and death for love of my love, encourage me to control myself and give Him love for love.

Sometimes the thought of His great humility in becoming man gives me the strength to control my pride.

Sometimes His example of poverty gives me the control I need not to procure or desire the things I cannot afford.

Sometimes His desire to accomplish His Father's Will, no matter how difficult, gives me the courage to mortify myself in order to do His Will.

Sometimes His silence, when He was accused unjustly, helps me control my tongue when I want to lash out in retaliation.

And sometimes when nothing else seems to work, I imagine the hurt look on His Face when Peter disappointed Him by his denial. I realize I too can cause Him to feel betrayed again by one He loves so deeply. I must control myself not only for my sake but most of all for His sake. He deserves my best.

Repentance leads to self-control and self-control proves my repentance. My sorrow for sin must stem from the realization that I have deeply hurt my Lord—a Lord who loves me as if no one else existed, who longingly waits for my return of love, and who reaches *out* to forgive immediately after an offense if only I reach *up* to seek it.

Unless I have a strong motive—a motive accompanied by His strength and love—my repentance will never bear the fruit of self-control.

I must Will to please Him no matter what the cost and He will not be outdone in generosity. His reward will be a hundred times greater than my effort deserves.

Repentance and self-control must go hand in hand. I will grow in them both because every day I fall short but every day I stand tall in His grace, and His grace is sufficient for me.

Prayer

Lord Jesus, be with me and give me your strength to overcome my weakness. Let my repentance bear the fruit of self-control that I may never willfully disappoint You or offend our Father.

Scripture

He has given us the guarantee of something very great and wonderful to come: through them you will be able to share the divine nature and to escape corruption in a world that is sunk in vice.

But to attain this, you will have to do your utmost yourselves, adding goodness to the faith that you have, understanding to your goodness, self-control to your understanding, patience to your self-control, true devotion to your patience, kindness towards your fellow men to your devotion, and, to this kindness, love.

If you have a generous supply of these, they will not leave you ineffective or unproductive.... But without them a man is blind or else short-sighted; he has forgotten how his past sins were washed away. (2 Pet. 1:4-8, 9)

DISCERNING AND JUDGING

In the Gospel of St. Luke, Jesus gives me directions on when to judge and when not to judge (Lk. 6:27-45).

He first encourages me to love my enemies, do good to them, bless them, and pray for them. He warns me that if I love only those who love me in return, I am no better than a pagan.

I am asked to imitate my Father who is kind to the ungrateful and wicked.

When Jesus made these statements He prepared the way to clarify what was to follow, for He asked me not to judge and then said I would be able to discern a person's integrity by his fruit.

He pressed this even further when He said that you do not gather figs from thorns or grapes from brambles, and a man's words flow out of what fills his heart.

I face what seems to be a contradiction — I am not to judge and yet I must judge.

Perhaps the Lord is telling me that I must *discern* the kind of fruit my brother bears and then judge whether or not it is worthy of imitation, or if it calls for my understanding and compassion.

I must have the humility and courage necessary to treat others as I wish they would treat me. When they take advantage of me or wish me harm, I am to pray for them and bless them.

In this case, I have not excluded them from my love.

The priority rests upon a simple command—I am to love my neighbor regardless of his actions. My love is not to be based on his goodness or my approval of his actions. It is to be based solely on the desire to imitate my Father, who is kind to the good and the wicked.

This means I love with a pure love, though I have no hope of return.

What I must discern in my neighbor is whether or not his actions or words are capable of separating me from God. This may be by his bad example, dishonest life, false doctrine, immorality, and many other ways that can deter me from the path of holiness.

The Lord said that from a bad tree comes bad fruit; in other words, I will be able to see this fruit in my brother's actions and I will know what it is that the Lord wishes me to do.

If it is good fruit, I am called upon by God to partake of the fruit of good example, by praising His Goodness and taking courage for my own life.

If it is bad fruit, I must not partake of that fruit or follow him in any way. I am expected to see a need in my brother, pray for him, not exclude him from my love, and do good to him should the occasion arise.

In this manner, the emphasis is not on my brother's actions but on my brother's needs. My concern is not to judge his motives but to pour the healing balm of kindness on his wounds. My obligation is to pray for him if he is wicked and not condemn him as being lost.

God in His Infinite Mercy constantly reaches out to the most wicked of men, offering forgiveness and grace. As long as a sinner lives, God will pursue him, and judge him only at death.

I must imitate my Father and realize that judgment is reserved for the hour of death and then it is rendered by God alone.

God expects me to be compassionate with the faults and sins of others, keeping in mind my own sins. He also expects me to be prudent and observe what kind of fruit my neighbor bears in order to praise God if it is good or to be compassionate if it is not.

I cannot judge a person's motives or decide whether or not he is or is not saved. I must have hope that God will give my brother every opportunity to be saved until his dying breath.

I am only to discern how his actions and example affect my life with God, love and pray for him, be he friend or foe, and let God judge his life and the state of his soul.

In this way I separate myself from my neighbor's interior and see him only as a brother whose life and example bring forth praise, or understanding and compassion.

I must understand this difference between discerning and judging.

To judge is to see a person's actions, form an opinion, and decide his motives. My decision as to his interior dispositions is based entirely on his exterior actions. This is to judge only half a man for I cannot see all the things that make him what he is at this moment.

A Court Judge who would judge a prisoner when only half the information was given would be unjust and unfair. The whole story may well acquit the prisoner. I would call such a judge biased and prejudiced.

This is why I cannot make final judgments about anyone, no matter how wicked. However, I must *discern* many times during my earthly sojourn, and it may be well to see how and what to look for, so that I may discern but not judge.

I must understand that there are three spirits to discern: the Holy Spirit, the human spirit, and the evil spirit.

It is not necessary to discern these spirits constantly, but there are times when it is necessary, so I will look at all three.

Discerning the Holy Spirit

The Holy Spirit brings inner peace. This does not exclude persecution or suffering. Many things the first Christians said and did brought upon them pain and anxiety. But because they were filled with the Holy Spirit they maintained joy and a conviction that the Lord was with them.

They bore the fruit of patience, love, kindness, goodness, mercy, and joy. This was their witness to the world that Jesus was Lord. It was their union with Him that converted pagans and made their neighbor realize they had something to give.

And so it is today. I will be able to observe that "something" in my neighbor's behavior and conduct that speaks a thousand words — something intangible but so visible that I desire to possess it too.

His Spirit in my neighbor seems to feed my soul by a glance, a word, or a smile. I somehow know it is the Lord.

The Human Spirit

Discerning the human spirit is easy at times and at other times difficult.

In my neighbor, it is easy because hypocrisy, lying, pride, jealousy, and greed are so obvious and although I cannot judge the source of these bad qualities, I can at least see them and be careful I do not fall into the same sins.

But in discerning the human spirit in my own soul it is difficult because in dealing with myself I must *judge* my *motives* and this necessitates self-knowledge.

The tables are somehow turned. With my neighbor I can discern his actions but cannot judge his interior motives. With myself I must judge my motives because I cannot see my actions as others see them.

I must discern what my spirit really is in relationship with God. I alone know why I do what I do and I must be honest enough to acknowledge, at least to God, my selfish or otherwise unchristian motives.

My human spirit seeks itself instead of God or neighbor. It excuses the most serious faults and becomes blind to any of its imperfections. I must realize this danger and be careful that my motives are always on a high spiritual level.

Perhaps this is what the Master meant when He said I must be careful not to take the splinter out of my brother's eye and forget the log in my own. Only when I see myself, He said, would I be able to help my brother.

I do not know the motives of my brother's actions, but what I do see, his exterior, constitutes the splinter that the Lord spoke of.

On the other hand, I know my own motives and my motives constitute the reason behind my actions. God judges my actions by my motives. This is the log that the Lord wants me to set right before I correct others.

When I fully know myself, purify my motives, and am careful that my desires and goals are geared toward God, then I will be able to help my brother. I can help him remove those specks in the eye of his soul that cloud his vision of God.

The Evil Spirit

The Tempter and his actions are easily observed by anyone who sincerely seeks God: there is a feeling of uneasiness that causes anxiety, unrest, and lack of peace.

The Tempter starts with pleasure and ends with pain. His road is easy, wide, and undisciplined. He promotes selfishness, pride, rudeness, anger, impatience, disobedience, and every other evil.

He offers pleasure for a moment but reserves the pain for Eternity. He is the father of lies and must be treated as such. He offers much but gives nothing.

Every day I must ask the Lord to give me His grace to withstand the onslaughts of the evil one, and His grace will be sufficient for me.

Prayer

Lord Jesus, instill within my soul a spirit of understanding that I may never rashly judge my neighbor. Let me examine my own motives and draw from Thy Heart the courage I need to change my own life before I help my brother change his life.

Scripture

In judging others you condemn yourself, since you behave no differently from those you judge. (Rom. 2:1)

There must be no passing of premature judgment. Leave that until the Lord comes: He will light up all that is hidden in the dark and reveal the secret intentions of men's hearts. (1 Cor. 4:5)

Brothers, if one of you misbehave, the more spiritual of you who set him right should do so in a spirit of gentleness, not forgetting that you may be tempted yourselves.... Let each of you examine his own conduct. (Gal. 6:1, 4)

My brothers, never grow tired of doing what is right. If anyone refuses to obey ... take note of him and have nothing to do with him so he will feel that he is in the wrong; though you are not to regard him as an enemy but as a brother in need of correction. (2 Thes. 3:13-15)

When self-indulgence is at work the results are obvious: fornication, gross indecency, and sexual irresponsibility;

idolatry and sorcery; feuds and wrangling, jealousy, bad temper and quarrels; disagreements, factions, envy, drunkenness, orgies, and similar things ... you who behave like this will not inherit the Kingdom.

Since the Spirit is our life, let us be directed by the Spirit. (Gal. 5:19-21, 25)

VALUE OF SUFFERING

One day Jesus said to His Apostles that He had come to bring fire to the earth. Then He explained the fire by saying that He had a baptism He was still to receive and He was in great distress until He had received it (Lk. 12:49-50). On another day, James and John, excited over the glory of the ministry and the popularity of their Master, asked to sit at the right and left of Jesus in His Kingdom (Mk. 10:37). Jesus told them they did not know what they were saying.

He then asked them a question, "Can you drink of the cup that I must drink, or be baptized with the baptism with which I must be baptized?" In their enthusiasm for honor and glory, they replied, "We can."

It was then that Jesus answered their question with a reply they did not wish to hear:

"The cup that I must drink you shall drink, and with the baptism with which I must be baptized you shall be baptized" (Mk. 10:38-39).

He would not promise them seats of honor in the Kingdom, for those were not His to give, but He would promise them suffering. They must look upon suffering as He did — as a baptism — a cleansing — something that renews, purifies, and transforms.

Suffering in any form was, from the beginning of time, a mystery, and a blot on the human race. It was feared, dreaded, and shunned — a sign of contradiction and a curse. Jesus came as man and, because He accepted the consequences of our fall and suffered as we all suffer, He elevated suffering, transformed it, gave it power, and considers the pain of each member of the human race His pain. So much so that when I alleviate the pain of my brother, or am compassionate with his ills, Jesus considers this done to Him.

There was suffering, pain, hunger, and thirst, before Redemption, and there is still suffering, pain, hunger, and thirst after Redemption. Redemption gave me more than an exemption from pain: it gave me Jesus, grace, the Spirit, love, peace, and joy. It raises me above pain.

God does not will that I suffer, just as He did not will that Adam and Eve sin. But since they sinned and I inherit the weaknesses that are the result of that sin, I do and always will have something to endure.

The world handled these weaknesses badly throughout the centuries, but God in His Infinite Mercy and Love sent His Son to take upon Himself these very weaknesses and to show me how to use the cross to my advantage.

The Prince of this world will always have his adherents pursue me as roaring lions; my physical and spiritual weakness will always beset me with ills and trials, but I need never fear. Jesus has conquered the world, and with Him in me, I too will conquer.

Christ's Redemption merited for me a participation in His Divine Nature as God through grace, and a participation in His sufferings as Man, through the Cross.

He came down from glory to my suffering level that I might rise from my misery to His Glory. But to do this I must take upon myself the whole Christ — suffering and resurrected. He took upon Himself my sins that I might sin no more.

He took upon Himself my weaknesses that I might have grace to overcome.

He took upon Himself my pain that I might hold his Hand in mine.

He took upon Himself my humiliation that I might be raised to His Throne.

He took upon Himself ridicule and insult that I might stand tall in persecution.

He took upon Himself the loss of His friends in His hour of need that I might never be alone in the hour of my need.

And then He stood alone, abandoned by God and man, so that I need never feel desolate or rejected.

How then can I ever think, even for a moment, that I can be transformed into a worthy son of God unless I follow in His Blood-stained Footsteps?

There are many kinds of suffering—physical, spiritual, mental, and temptations, but regardless of the source of suffering it can be meritorious.

Even the suffering I bring upon myself by my own faults and weaknesses, can all be turned into grace and merit.

It is wonderful to realize that what was a consequence of sin can become an occasion of merit.

Christ suffers in me and in my neighbor and that suffering brings forth from me patience, compassion, love, and many other qualities that only the hammer of pain can forge.

I have only to look at Scripture to see the difference between pain before Christ and after Christ.

In the Old Testament, the very Cross He died on was considered a curse. The Messiah was not recognized or accepted, because He chose to live a common life and die an ignominious death — a death that was a scandal to His own people and sheer nonsense to the pagans.

One day He said He did not come to bring peace but the sword. His redemption was not to restore the preternatural qualities we lost when Adam and Eve sinned.

No, Jesus would do more than that. He would elevate suffering, and the curse, turned into the Cross, bears the fruit of a new life — a resurrected life begun here and continued forever in Eternity.

St. Paul was very conscious of this new aspect of suffering — the suffering that brings joy because it has a purpose. He said to the Romans one day that we can boast about looking forward to God's glory but that wasn't all we can boast about: "... we can boast about our suffering. These sufferings bring patience, as we know, and patience brings perseverance, and perseverance brings hope, and this hope is not deceptive, because the love of God has been poured into our hearts by the Holy Spirit which has been given us" (Rom. 5:4-6).

After Jesus came and suffered, Paul saw it all in a new light. Now there was a purpose to it all—suffering was no longer a curse, a burden, an unbearable yoke; it was all *His* burden, *His* yoke.

Now it is *our* cross—His and mine.

Now there is a reason behind each tear, each pain, each heartache.

Now the cross is no longer in the mud of despair—it is raised on high and on it is God's own Son.

Now it is no longer a sign of His vengeance but a sign of His love.

Now it no longer destroys but molds and renews.

Now it no longer oppresses my spirit but empties it so that it may be filled with God.

For each heartache empties my soul of me and fills it with Him.

Each tear washes my soul and makes it more beautiful to His Eyes.

Each disappointment strengthens my will to cling to Him alone.

Each anxious day makes me look to Him for support.

Each tension-filled hour makes me reach out to find serenity in His grasp.

Each pain is added to His on the Cross to redeem the world.

Each doubt makes me search for Truth and hold it fast.

Each separation gives me an awareness of the one thing necessary.

Each time my love is spurned I know how He feels when I ignore Him.

Each time I am treated unjustly I know His feelings when He was called a devil.

Each time pride, jealousy, or ambition rears its head I see His Crown of Thorns.

Yes, the Father uses my brother's imperfections, the temptations of the evil one, and my own weaknesses to prune me of those qualities in my soul that are so unlike Him. He even uses the wickedness of men to prune me and bear witness to others.

There is an example of this in St. Luke's Gospel. People had come to tell Jesus how Pilate had killed some Galileans and mixed their blood with the sacrifice to the pagan gods. Jesus, knowing what the people were thinking, said, "Do you suppose these Galileans who suffered like that were greater sinners than any other Galileans? They were not. No; but unless you repent you will all perish as they did" (Luke 13:2-3).

Here is an answer to many problems that concern the suffering of the innocent.

Jesus was saying that those who suffer unjustly are martyrs —they are not being punished for some great or hidden sin. But their unjust death must be an example of how depraved human nature can become. I must do all I can to eradicate the poverty, ignorance, and greed that cause men to treat their brothers so unjustly. It calls for repentance—both mine and my brother's—or we will perish together. I must rejoice with those who suffer for the sake of the Kingdom for their reward is great. But I must also pray for their persecutors that they may repent and be forgiven.

It is said in the Acts of the Apostles that Peter and John rejoiced when they were flogged and humiliated for the sake of His Name (Acts 5:40-41).

The language of the Cross is illogical to the worldly minded, but to those who seek the wisdom of God and salvation, it is God's power to save (1 Cor. 1:18).

Paul reminds me in his Epistle to the Corinthians that both suffering and consolation overflow to me from Christ. Because it is all a part of Him, it has the power to give support and consolation to others in their trials (2 Cor. 1:5).

It was the powerful witness of patient and joyful suffering that converted pagans and made them realize that Christianity could make something that was ugly into something beautiful to behold.

I must accept the daily splinters He gives me from His Cross as precious jewels in my future crown.

Like all the mysteries of God, pain and suffering are something I shall never fully understand. I can be sure, however, that if Jesus chose such a large portion of it for Himself, I must follow in His Footsteps.

I can trust His judgment as to the kind and size of the cross best suited to my shoulders.

The cross prepares my soul for the glory to come. "Yes, the troubles which are soon over, though they weigh little, train us for the carrying of a weight of eternal glory which is out of proportion to them" (2 Cor. 4:17).

The cross detaches me from worldly things, and instills within my soul a desire for the Homeland. "So we have no eyes for things that are visible, but only for things that are invisible; for visible things last only for a time, and the invisible things are eternal" (2 Cor. 4:18).

The cross, my concept of suffering, and the way I accept it, all prove to my neighbor that I am a Christian. "We prove we are servants of God by great fortitude in times of suffering, in times of hardship and distress;... prepared for honor or disgrace, for blame or praise ... thought most miserable and yet always rejoicing" (2 Cor. 6:4, 8, 10).

The cross is a sign of His love. "It would be a sign from God that He has given you the privilege not only of believing in Christ, but of suffering for Him as well" (Phil. 1:29). The cross is a great aid in the development of my union with God. "My brothers, you will always have your trials, but, when they come, try to treat them as a happy privilege; you understand that your faith is only put to the test to make you patient,... so that you will become fully developed, complete, with nothing missing" (James 1:2-3, 4).

The cross makes me compassionate with the faults and temptations of my brother. "It was appropriate that God should make perfect, through suffering, the Leader—so that by His death He could take away the power of the devil.... It was essential that He should in this way become completely like His brothers so that He could be compassionate ... because He has Himself been through temptation, He is able to help others who are tempted" (Heb. 2:10, 17-18). The cross teaches me how to obey for "although He was Son, He learnt to obey through suffering" (Heb. 5:8).

The cross is a sign of sonship. "My son, when the Lord corrects you, do not treat it lightly, but do not get discouraged when He reprimands you. For the Lord trains the ones He loves and He punishes all those that He acknowledges as His sons. Suffering is part of your training. God is treating you as His sons" (Heb. 12:5-6). The cross in the form of bodily pain caused by sickness or the struggle to live a Christian life, unites me to God's Will. "Think of what Christ suffered in this life, and then arm yourselves with the same resolution that He had: anyone who in this life has bodily suffering has broken with sin, because for the rest of his life he is not ruled by human passions but only by the Will of God" (1 Pet. 4:1-2).

The cross is essential for union with Christ. "I have been crucified with Christ, and I live now not with my own life but with the life of Christ, who lives in me" (Gal. 2:20).

The cross is a powerful means of mortifying my self-indulgence and a proof to my neighbor that I am sincere in striving for holiness. "You cannot belong to Christ Jesus unless you crucify all self-indulgent passions and desires.... The only thing I can boast about is the Cross of our Lord Jesus Christ, through whom the world is crucified to me, and I to the world" (Gal. 5:24, 6:14).

The Cross makes me worthy of God. "Anyone who does not take his cross and follow in my footsteps is not worthy of me" (Mt. 10:38).

Prayer

Lord Jesus, let me appreciate the crosses in my life that I may reap the fruit of their burden and be a true son of the Father.

Confidence, Trust, and Abandonment

Jesus called His Apostles to Him and gave them a discourse on what to expect in their ministry. Though He gave them power over spirits and diseases, He warned them that they would not always be accepted. Their portion in life would be, for the most part, persecution.

They were to go on their journey without money, armed only with the *confidence* that He would provide. They were to *trust* Him and cure all that came to them freely because everything was given to them without charge. They were to *abandon* themselves to His Providence completely and go from house to house to bring peace. But in those homes that did not receive their peace, they were told to shake the dust off their feet and not permit the rebuff to enter their souls. God would take care (Mt. 10).

Jesus always "told it like it is." He never promised me it would be easy but He did say my burden would be light provided my trust in Him was complete and He and I bore our yoke together.

There seems to be three degrees of hope in the tenth chapter of St. Matthew.

The first is to have *confidence* that God *can* do all things —this is to ask.

The second is to have *trust* that God *will* give me what I need—this is to seek.

The third is to *abandon* myself to His time—and this is to knock.

I will look at all three degrees to see how I may grow in hope.

Confidence — To Ask

When Jesus told the Apostles to cure the sick as they went on their journey and not to carry a purse, or haversack, or spare tunics, He was building up their confidence in His Providence.

The power to help those in need came directly from Him and they were not to depend upon anything but Him to sustain them.

My temperament and culture are different than theirs, but the principle is the same.

The command to go out and do such great things, with so little to fall back on, must have seemed difficult indeed.

But this is the beginning of being completely filled with Jesus. I must understand that His Hand guides every facet of my life.

He was telling His Apostles that even those mundane things like food and clothing are provided by Him.

How often in my life have I thought that God was not interested in my daily needs — the kind of needs that keep me warm and my stomach filled? It is a big mistake if I relegate God's interest in me to spiritual things only. He is completely interested in my whole person and in everything that concerns it. Nothing is too small and nothing too great.

I can ask for anything, from good weather to cancer cure, from hitting a home run to finding a job, from peace of mind to joy of heart. Yes, I can discuss anything, tell Him anything, and ask for anything, and have the confidence that He hears and cares.

The only thing He asks is that after I have expressed my needs I do not continue to carry them around like clothing —encumbering my journey home.

After I have asked—asked for anything—He has heard.

Confidence permits me to speak to God as a child. It assures me that He is deeply interested in everything that concerns me. It is a deep awareness of that concern—an awareness that brings peace.

I cannot shut Him out of a large part of my life with the excuse that He is not interested in the simple and mundane things of my daily existence.

He said one day that not a hair falls from my head that He does not know it (Mt. 10:29-30). He wanted me to know that His concern goes that far so I can be confident that He is interested in little things.

My confidence in God must be the kind that assures me in every circumstance that He *can* do anything for me. It gives me the courage to ask with childlike simplicity—a quality that asks and then goes its way in peace.

This leads to the next step and that is, to trust. To trust is to realize that God *will* do everything that is in my best interest.

Trust — To Seek

There are times in my life when God's Will is not clear. I must seek that Will the best way I know.

I seek it through prayer, reading, advice, and past experience. Here is where trust must be manifested.

Trust assures me that when I seek His Will to the best of my ability, He accepts whatever the result may be — success or failure — and I may be at peace.

I must trust that He ...

- forgives and forgets my sins,
- understands my desires,
- knows the secret aspirations of my heart,
- sees the effort that ends in failure,
- knows I'm innocent though accused guilty,
- will take care of me in the future,
- sees how hard it is to overcome myself,
- is aware of every disappointment and heartache,
- and will bring good out of every pain and sorrow.

When I trust God, I am telling Him that I am completely confident that He *will do* whatever is for my good.

As long as I do all in my power to lead a Christian life, I can leave everything else to Him because it is a lack of trust that makes me wonder if I am making any progress.

A lack of trust makes me put more emphasis on seeing my fruit rather than on bearing fruit.

A lack of trust makes me doubt His love when I ask for one thing and receive another.

A lack of trust makes me forget His Providence in the past and doubt His Providence in the future.

A lack of trust makes me dissatisfied with my present lot —thinking the grass is greener on the other side.

A lack of trust makes me think that holiness is for other people but not for me.

A lack of trust makes me think He doesn't care.

A lack of trust makes me look upon the sufferings in my life as useless.

Yes, a lack of trust makes me think God *can* help me but won't.

I must seek the good in everything in order to increase my trust in God.

I must meditate often on His Attributes and realize that if He looks after the sparrow, how much more will He look after me.

To trust completely is often to wait, and this brings me to the third step — abandonment.

Abandonment — To Knock

To abandon myself to God means I trust Him to such a degree that I am satisfied with *everything* He does in my life. I am free of the burden of waiting for the answer to my prayer.

My prayer is made with a loving certainty that God has heard and will take care. It is the kind of prayer that has no hesitation.

This prayer of abandonment is one in which I give myself, and all that belongs to me, into His loving care.

I can go my way knowing that if I seek the Kingdom first, all the rest will be added.

The word "abandon" means I leave my needs in God's Hands.

I do not worry about how or when He answers my petitions. As a child of so loving a Father, I realize He desires my good more than I do.

This abandon is especially needed when I must wait for an answer or the answer I receive is not to my liking.

God created me to know Him and love Him, and all the things I ask for must be for the fulfillment of that plan.

His love for me is so great, His knowledge of my future so perfect, that He knows exactly what is good for me.

I must keep this in mind when I do not receive the things I ask for.

If He sees best not to give me what I ask, I may be sure that He will give me something better.

A deep realization of the next life will be a great help in giving myself totally into His care.

In God's mind everything in my life must have some significance for the next life. Everything here must add to my glory there.

In this way I increase my happiness in eternity, but most important, I increase His Glory, meaning that for all eternity I will glorify His Mercy and Love in my regard, for All of Heaven to see.

I must take the same long range view of all the events in my life as God does. I must measure each event in the light of eternity and be willing to forego or wait for anything.

I limit His Power and my future happiness when I insist on my own will or become bitter when things do not go my way.

I ask with *confidence*, I seek in *trust*, and I knock and wait at the door of His Heart in *abandonment*.

Prayer

Lord Jesus, ask the Father to give me the confidence of a child, the trust of a son, and the abandon of a lover, that I may always live in the Shadow of His Spirit.

Scripture

CONFIDENCE

We are bold enough to approach God in complete confidence, through our faith in Him; so I beg you, never lose confidence just because of the trials that I go through on your account: they are your glory. (Eph. 3:12-13)

We are quite confident that if we ask Him for anything, and it is in accordance with His Will, He will hear us: and knowing that whatever we may ask, He hears us, we know that we have already been granted what we asked of Him. (1 Jn. 5:14-15)

TRUST

Trust Him, and He will uphold you. Follow a straight path and hope in Him.... You who fear the Lord, trust Him, and you will not be baulked of your reward. (Sir. 2:6, 8)

ABANDONMENT

Whatever happens to you, accept it, and in the uncertainty of your humble state, be patient, since gold is tested in the fire, and chosen men in the furnace of humiliation.... You who fear the Lord, wait for His Mercy; do not turn aside in case you fall. (Sir. 2:4-5, 7)

COURAGE

One night as Jesus was asleep in Simon's boat, a gale began to blow and the waves were breaking into the boat. The Apostles were frightened and Jesus was asleep in the stern of the boat.

They went to Jesus and said, "Master, do you not care? We are going down!" Jesus awoke, quieted the storm, and made a strange statement. He said to the storm, "Quiet now! Be calm," and to the Apostles, "Why are you so frightened? How is it that you have no faith?" (Mark 4:35-41).

Why did Jesus correct them for being frightened? Surely it was a human reaction—the waves were breaking into the boat and they were sinking.

Were they frightened of the storm? These men were professional fishermen and had weathered many storms. The type of fear they experienced was the kind that lacked confidence and courage. It was the fear that He did not care.

Their question tells me the kind of fear they possessed, and this kind of fear is more than human fear — it is spiritual fear, a fear that paralyzes the soul by instilling the thought that God is asleep and doesn't care.

They had not lost their faith that He was God else they would not have asked a sleeping man if He didn't care. They knew that as God, asleep or awake, He was aware of their plight.

Their fright stemmed entirely from the conviction that He knew but did not care.

This is the essence of courage: to stand tall though afraid, in the midst of life's storms, realizing that He knows and cares.

I may be afraid — that is human — but realizing He cares, while I accept the pain of the storm, is superhuman — it is courageous.

There are many "good" fears in life — fears that help me advance in holiness.

There is ...

- the filial fear that prevents me from offending God,
- the fear that makes me cautious in times of danger,
- the fear that makes me resist things that may harm my life,
- the fear that makes me preserve my health,

- the fear of offending a loved one,
- the fear of failure that often gives me the perseverance to be a success,
- the fear that bids me stay away from occasions of sin lest I fall,
- the fear that is born of prudence and tells me when an act of bravery is courageous or foolhardy,
- the fear that prevents me from making a fool out of myself by doing more than my talents permit.

These are "good" kinds of fear because the fruit they bear is good; they preserve life and love, and promote my spiritual growth.

However, there are times in my life when other fears grip my soul and their fruit destroys and crushes.

This kind is not the natural human fear but the kind that is spiritual — born of weak faith and knowledge of God — fear that is sowed by the Tempter, who seeks to destroy.

- This fear centers my thoughts on me, on my capabilities, on my strength, and on my power. It weighs all these things, finds them wanting and then despairs.
- It convinces me that I can do nothing even with His Power behind me.

- It sees only darkness in the past, clouds in the present, and storms in the future.
- It disturbs everyone and is suspicious of everything.
- It convinces my soul that nothing can or will be done about my problems or difficulties.
- It promotes dissatisfaction with those around me as if they were solely responsible for my state.
- It nourishes insecurity and makes me feel I am not worthy to do or become anything worthwhile.
- It eats at the heart of my soul by telling me that He has not forgiven my sins—not really.
- It covers me like a dark blanket—blotting out all joy and peace—a heavy burden that smothers His life out of my soul.

These kinds of fear, born of the Deceiver, cripple every action, dampen every desire, and cloud every light that Jesus tries to shine on my soul.

These kinds of fears are the kind I must conquer by prayer, humility, and a deeper faith. I must cling to His Cross and Promises as an anchor of Hope to stabilize my emotions and calm my troubled soul.

Courage is impossible with these kinds of fear because my soul is incapable of exerting the strength necessary to be courageous.

Real spiritual courage is often accompanied by a healthy fear. It is this good fear that makes me most courageous because it pushes me forward with prudence.

Prudence is that quality that determines when I am being courageous or presumptuous.

Prudence brings to mind that it often takes more courage to retreat and rest for a future battle than to go on depending on myself and ending up a failure.

I must be stout-hearted and trust in the Lord to accomplish His Will, love my neighbor, bear my burdens, and look to the future with confidence.

Jesus was afraid in the Garden of Gethsemane — His human nature recoiled from the sufferings to come and the realization that in spite of His Love many would reject Him.

It was enough to make God's Son afraid, but that very fear made His determination to accomplish His Father's Will more courageous.

The degree of His fear, and the intensity of His Love, determined the heroism of His courage.

I must look at courage in this new light: it is a good fear coupled with determination, trust in His Power, and a love for His Will.

No matter how afraid I am, as long as I do what He is asking me to do, I can rest assured—I have been courageous.

Prayer

Lord Jesus, there are many times that fear grips my soul. Cast your shadow around me and let me face life unafraid.

Scripture

Strengthen all weary hands, steady all trembling knees, and say to all faint hearts, "Courage. Do not be afraid." (Is. 35:3-4)

God Himself has said: I will not fail you or desert you, and so we can say with confidence: "With the Lord to help me, I fear nothing: what can man do against me?" (Heb. 13:5-6)

Courage

Then Jesus came with them to a small estate called Gethsemane.... And sadness came over Him, and great distress. Then He said to them, "My soul is sorrowful to the point of death." ... "My Father," He said, "if it is possible, let this cup pass me by. Nevertheless, let it be as You, not I, would have it.".... "Get up! Let us go — My betrayer is already close at hand." (Mt. 26:36, 37-38, 39, 46)

THE CHRISTIAN DILEMMA

As I read Scripture to find solutions to problems, guidance for decisions, forgiveness for my sins, and consolation in times of distress, I find contradictions.

I find one passage that seems to solve my problem, only to find another that, on the surface at least, cancels out what I thought was the answer to my need.

I am faced with a dilemma: positives and negatives — pros and cons.

I will look at some of these dilemmas and try to find a criterion by which I can join opposites together to give me the whole picture of Christian living.

Dilemma 1

I am told in Chapter 6 of St. Matthew that I should love my enemies, and pray for those who persecute me, because the

Father lets His sun rise on the good and the bad. I am told further that if I do not love my enemies I am no better than the pagans who love only those who love them.

But in Chapters 16 and 23 I am asked to "Beware of the yeast of the Pharisees and Sadducees" (Mt. 16:6). He pronounces seven woes upon them—woes that are frightening to read. A person with the character of a Pharisee is certainly an enemy, and yet I am told to love and beware.

If I read the two separately I find a dilemma, but when I read them together I find a solution.

I am to love all men—sinner and saint alike. Neither one should occupy my mind to the point where they interfere with my own union with God, for both are sustained by God and both can switch places at any time; a saint may become a sinner, and a sinner, a saint.

God lets His sun (grace) shine on both until they make their last decision—for or against Him—at death. In the meantime, I must be good to my brother and wish him well.

But while the sinner is a sinner, I am not to follow his example. I must call a spade a spade, and not pretend a sinner may be a hidden saint.

If that person is in the position of authority, I am to do what he says (provided it is not against God's Commandments), but I am not to be guided by his actions.

A bad tree bears bad fruit, but I must be content that the Lord and Master permits it to continue growing with the hope that it will at some time, after much pruning, bear good fruit.

To wait and be patient until that time arrives is to love an enemy. To continue bearing good fruit in my own life, in the face of bad fruit, is to beware of the enemy.

Here I must make a distinction between bad people and evil people.

A brother may do bad things through weakness — adultery, stealing, drinking, etc. — and though I cannot judge his motives I can see his need and manifest my concern by prayer and good example. I must stay away from these occasions of sin lest I fall as my brother has fallen.

These bad things in a brother's life can constitute him an enemy to me and to God.

Here is where I need compassion and love. Jesus showed me this many times in His treatment of sinners. He came to heal the sick in soul, and His Love and Compassion gave them the courage to repent and reform.

Though their bad lives offended God and hurt other people, their real motive was not to offend but to give in to their selfish and self-indulgent passions.

They are sick in soul, many unaware of the gravity of their sickness, bent upon one thing alone: self-satisfaction. They are not interested in the souls of others, only in pleasure.

To this kind of enemy I must be kind as my Father is kind, pray for them, and help them.

But Jesus warns me of other enemies of whom I must be aware and stay away from, the kind of enemy who is evil—the brother who promotes immorality, the prophet who preaches false doctrine, the hypocrite who acts good only to destroy.

The neighbor who seeks to destroy my faith, my God, my goodness, my ideals, and my love, is evil.

The neighbor who tells me there is nothing to come—"Eat, drink, and be merry, for tomorrow we die"—that man is evil.

A brother can offend my feelings, crush my pride, desert me in times of need, but his actions can help build me up by patient endurance—so I can love him, pray for him, and wish him well.

But if he seeks to snatch away my soul, then I must beware. I can still pray for him as Jesus did, but I must not permit him to influence my life. This is what is meant by "staying away."

His evil influence does not touch me; it is separated from me by the shield of faith and perseverance.

The solution to the problem is in our Lord's statement to beware of the yeast of the Pharisee type of enemy.

Yeast is the spirit of the dough — it builds it up into a loaf.

The yeast of an enemy that is bad can help me grow in virtue when I imitate my Father who is kind to all.

But the yeast of an enemy who is evil is destructive — it sours the dough and makes it worthy only to be thrown away.

I must then put up with a bad enemy and stay away from an evil enemy.

Dilemma 2

In the 5th Chapter of St. Matthew, Jesus tells me that the peacemakers are blest — so blest, that they shall be called children of God.

But in the 10th Chapter of Matthew, He says He did not come to bring peace but the sword. He came to set a man against his father, a daughter against her mother.

In the 22nd Chapter of St. Luke, He told His Apostles that, before, he sent them out without purse or sandals — but now, they were to take purse and haversack, and if they had no sword, they were to sell their cloaks and buy one.

But in the 26th Chapter of Matthew, when Peter took his sword and cut off the servant's ear, Jesus told Peter to put up his sword, for those who live by the sword will die by the sword.

Jesus is the Prince of Peace, but neither in His life nor in mine is that peace dependent upon the absence of turmoil. The peace that comes from God is dependent upon the sword of mortification and self-denial.

Jesus came to set me at war with myself. I am called upon every day to fight against the flesh, the world, and the devil. In this battle to live a Christian life, I may be opposed by those nearest and dearest to me — parents and family.

The moment Jesus came, He began to divide the Kingdom of Light from the Kingdom of Darkness.

By becoming man He showed me exactly what the Father expects from me. The knowledge of what He is, what I am, and what I should be, is the battleground on which two forces seek my soul.

The one force calls me to the heights and Divine Adoption. The other force calls me to the depths and darkness.

The one force bids me travel a narrow path strewn with crosses but ending in supreme bliss. The other force bids me travel a broad way strewn with pleasure but ending in misery.

The one force calls me to love my neighbor for himself; the other force tells me to love my neighbor for myself.

The one force demands faith in the invisible reality; the other force tells me there is no invisible reality.

The one force bids me do violence to myself for the sake of peace; the other force bids me create violence and then cry for peace.

The one force puts the emphasis on the glory in the next life; the other force puts the emphasis on the glory of this life.

The one force bids me find perfect peace in meekness and humility; the other force bids me find temporary peace at any cost—pride, ambition, anger, and lording it over others.

Yes, I must sell the cloak of selfishness and buy the sword of penance to cut away the world, pride, and the Tempter. The sword of the Spirit is the sword that helps prune me of those qualities that are not Christ-like.

As long as I think as Peter did—that the sword is something exterior that I wield on others, I will lose the meaning of His coming and the price of His peace.

I am to use every means at my disposal—poverty or riches, success or failure, praise or blame—all must be used to build, mold, prune, and shape me into another Christ.

The blade of the sword is His Spirit, pruning my soul, that it may hold the treasure of His Presence.

Dilemma 3

I am commanded by God to honor my father and mother and to love my neighbor as myself.

But in the 10th Chapter of St. Matthew, Jesus tells me that if I prefer my father or mother to Him, I am not worthy of Him.

I am to honor my parents whose love brought me into the world.

I am to respect them as two people who were chosen by God to give me a body into which He would breathe a soul.

I am to care for them in all their needs to the best of my ability.

I am to obey them as I would God, for they take His place during my earthly sojourn.

I am to be compassionate with their ills, and understanding with their problems.

I am to have a special love for them, unlike any other love.

But neither my parents nor anyone else can ever be permitted to deter me from following the commands of God, who is Lord, Creator, and Eternal Father.

He does not ask that He be my only love, but my first love.

All love that is not founded in Him will be selfish and temporary.

I must be willing to give up anyone or anything that may separate me from God for all eternity.

Here I must understand that even parents may try to keep me from following Jesus, but many times it is only because they do not have the same light as I have.

My love for them must be strong enough to be patient with their opposition until they receive the light to see God as I see Him.

Though my love for them remains steadfast, their opposition can never keep me from His side.

And this applies to brothers, sisters, relatives, and friends. I must love them all deeply, but if I am ever asked to make a choice, I must prefer Him to all of them.

I must be sure, however, that the choice is between parents and God, and not between parents and me.

Jesus warned me of this when He called the Pharisees hypocrites for saying that a man was not obliged to keep his father or mother, provided the money to be used for that purpose was given to the Temple (Mark 7:9-13).

This attitude exempted them from the sacrifice that concern demands, and salved their consciences by giving the money to God.

Hypocrisy is an evil and must be avoided at any cost. The point Jesus is making is that I must prefer God to myself, family, friends, land, and possessions—interiorly by loving Him above all things, and exteriorly, by loving all things in Him.

My obligations to my parents and neighbor can be fulfilled only when God is the center of my life. Then my devotion will be built on sacrifice and I will treat them as I would treat God.

Dilemma 4

In the 16th Chapter of St. Mark, Jesus tells me that there are certain signs by which Christians will be known: they will cast out devils, have different tongues, and will lay their hands on the sick, who will recover.

But in the 7th Chapter of St. Matthew, Jesus says that not all those who say, "Lord, Lord" will enter the Kingdom. And when the day comes and they say to Him, "Lord, Lord, did we not prophesy in Your Name, cast out demons in Your Name, work many miracles in Your Name?" Then He will tell them to their faces that He never knew them. He will say, "Away from Me you evil men" (Mt. 7:21-23).

This is difficult, because casting out demons and healing the sick looks like good fruit. In fact, this very power was given to the Apostles, and these signs proved to the pagans that the words spoken by the Apostles were anointed by the Lord.

Yet, Jesus calls some men who do these things evil men, and goes further by saying He never knew them.

I am reminded of the time Moses went before Pharaoh and performed marvels only to watch the Pharaoh's pagan prophets do the same.

I must plumb the depths of this mystery so that I am not deceived by fruit that looks good but is not good.

I notice, in reading of the signs and miracles performed by the Apostles, that they possessed a kind of nonchalance. They never seemed wrapped up in the fact that Jesus had given them the power to do great things. They were so absorbed in Jesus, and in spreading His Word, that the gifts were looked upon merely as tools to accomplish their mission.

All Christians throughout the centuries who were given great gifts, seemed to possess this same kind of humility.

Though many will come performing great marvels, even though they use His Name, unless they possess His humility they will not belong to Him.

The fruit of authentic signs is to focus the attention of the observer on God. The fruit of a sign not born of God, is to focus all the attention on the performer.

Signs and miraculous gifts are only leaves on the vine: the fruit is the important part.

The leaves add to its beauty, but without the fruit of proven virtue the vine is of no value.

I am reminded in St. John's Gospel that every vine that does not bear fruit the Father will gather together to burn. Jesus also said it is He in me who bears fruit.

When Jesus performed His miracles, they were only signs of His Sonship. He never lost sight of His real mission: to merit our pardon, to spread the Good News, and to call sinners to repentance.

To know Jesus and to be known by Him is to permit Him to bear fruits of love, compassion, mercy, and kindness in my life.

Charismatic gifts may be the added dimension needed to enliven faith in weak souls, but they never touch the essence of holiness—and that is, to be Jesus to my neighbor.

There are three kinds of charisma: natural, evil, and God-given.

A natural charism, such as the sparkling personality of a celebrity, will direct my attention to that person but may never benefit my soul.

An evil charism, such as that possessed by a dictator, attracts people to follow him, but bears only the fruit of discord and hate.

A God-given charism, often unknown or unnoticed by the receiver, as in the case of Pope John, attracts people to God, as they praise His Power in weak human beings.

A charism must bear the fruit of holiness in the one who receives it and promote faith, repentance, and a desire for God in those who witness it.

Without a decrease of self in the disciple, and an increase of Jesus, the Lord will truly say on the last day, "I know you not."

I must keep my soul united to Jesus that I may discern the right kind of fruit in my neighbor that I may praise His Providence, and bear the right kind of fruit in my soul that I may praise His Mercy.

MAKING CHOICES

In daily life I discern one thing: there are two kingdoms, the kingdom of light and the kingdom of darkness.

There are two ways: the way of virtue and the way of evil.

There are two paths: the narrow path that ends in eternal bliss, and the broad path that ends in misery.

There are two Princes who seek my soul: the Prince of Peace and the Prince of Darkness.

I must often stop during my journey home and take account of which of the two I choose the most.

As a Christian, I have the happy privilege of giving my total self to Jesus that He may bear fruit in my soul.

I am His ambassador to the world. He wants my eyes to see, my voice to speak, my hands to assure, and my feet to walk the path of holiness.

He seeks to bear fruit in my soul that the Father may be glorified.

He takes pleasure in my weakness that His Power may be manifest.

He desires to rest in my heart as in a temple where He reigns supreme over all.

He finds solace in my striving and comfort in my victories.

His Mercy thunders throughout the heavens when I ask forgiveness and His Justice is silent when I deserve His wrath.

He hovers over me as a mother over her only child, and gives me freedom to accept or reject Him.

He came, died, and rose for my sake, so that I will live, bear fruit, and die to myself for His sake.

The fruit I bear is the result of the choices I make. There are then, two criteria to go by: choices and fruit.

A good tree, the Master said, cannot bear bad fruit; neither can a bad tree bear good fruit.

Every choice I make between the two kingdoms forms some kind of fruit. When the choices are habitually good, I begin to resemble Jesus.

If the choices are habitually bad, I will acquire bad dispositions and the image of Jesus will be faint or entirely wiped away, as in the case of serious sin.

Though repentance renews my friendship with God it must not end there. Goodness is a growing process that results not in just one fruit, but many fruits.

I must daily strive, with the help of His grace, to change from mediocrity to great zeal, from lukewarmness to burning love, from impatience to patience, from selfishness to generosity, from fear to courage, from doubts to faith, and from despair to hope.

I must put on the mind of Christ, as St. Paul says, and see things as He desires to see them in me.

Prayer

Lord Jesus, let me live in You every moment of my life. Bear fruit in my soul, that together, we may glorify the Father through the power of His Spirit.

Scripture

Make your home in Me, as I make Mine in you.... Whoever remains in Me, with Me in him, bears fruit in plenty, for cut off from Me you can do nothing.

It is to the glory of My Father that you should bear much fruit, and then you will be My disciples.

... I commissioned you to go out and to bear fruit, fruit that will last, and then the Father will give you anything you ask in My Name. (Jn. 15:4, 5, 8, 16)

In His
Sandals

MEDITATION ON THE LIFE OF JESUS

He Emptied Himself

Jesus left the glory of Heaven to come down and take upon Himself a nature like my own, because He loves me so much.

I wonder if I understand how much of a humiliation it was for Jesus to become human. If being with the Father is something beyond our wildest dreams, just imagine what being equal to God must be like! How could He leave such a position for me?

I am ungrateful most of the time, and I prefer myself, people, and things to Him almost constantly. I don't have much to leave and yet I cling to the little I have as if I were never going to lose it.

What Did Jesus Do for Me?

He left Eternity and lived in Time that I might leave Time and live in Eternity.

He left the Eternal Father in all His Glory to come down as man and acknowledge the Father's supremacy over all mankind.

He came as a humble servant, to make reparation for those who say, "I will not serve."

He was lowly of heart and gave credit to the Father for everything He did, and offered His self-effacement as an atonement for my pride and independence.

He was Master of all but never imposed on anyone or forced them to follow Him.

His humility was so great that He understood the hatred of His enemies and asked His Father to forgive them.

He ruled all creation and yet subjected Himself to Joseph and Mary as an obedient son.

He was content to be considered an uneducated carpenter, yet He created the whole world.

He was subject to two people whom He created because He saw His Father's Will in their commands.

He was the Splendor of the Father, but He hid all that would distinguish Him from the rest of the children of men.

He was Uncreated Wisdom, but He did not disdain learning ordinary things from others.

He was content to advance in wisdom and age before men that I might be patient in advancing in holiness before God.

He accepted hatred, jealousy, and persecution with composure, seeing only the Father's Will in the plan of Redemption.

He was not ashamed to eat with sinners even though doing so belittled Him in the eyes of others.

He watched those He came to redeem abandon Him in His hour of need, without becoming bitter or resentful.

He extended to Peter a forgiving glance even before the Apostle was conscious of his sin.

He did not give up His Spirit until He had endured every possible torment — to prove His Love for me.

He rose from the grave and appeared first to Magdalene, a repentant sinner, to Peter who denied Him, and to the Disciples going to Emmaus whose faith was weak — to show that He understood their frailties and would not crush the bruised reed.

His Love for me was so deep that He could not bear leaving me alone, so He humbled Himself completely and gave me His Precious Body and Blood in the Holy Eucharist as food for my soul.

Love for Love

I look at the Incarnation with awe when I see Jesus conceal His Eternal Wisdom, Power, and Majesty, and assume human nature — not as an adult, but as an infant, totally dependent upon two of His creatures.

What would make Him do such a thing? The only answer is *Love* because only love is strong enough to overcome every obstacle. It is difficult to think of His Majesty and Power as obstacles — and yet they seemed to be. As God, there was no way to identify Himself with me. He knew I would often be tempted to look at Him and say, "How do You know what it feels like to suffer pain, failure, weakness, humiliations, hunger, and thirst?"

Now He Knows

He was satisfied with only a few people — Shepherds and Wise Men — knowing He came into the world.

He waited patiently for Mary to feed Him, and Joseph to provide for Him — yet, as God, He fed and sustained them both.

He refused to use His Power to annihilate Herod. Instead, He fled into Egypt with only Joseph and Mary for protection.

He waited until time took its course and Herod died before He returned to His own country.

At the age of twelve, He had the courage to do His Father's Will by remaining in the Temple, even though He knew His absence would cause untold agony to His parents. He wanted to teach me that God and the work of God must always come first.

Hidden Life

For thirty years, Jesus never allowed His Divinity to manifest itself. He was infinitely superior to everyone around Him but He never showed it.

He spent thirty of the thirty-three years (91% of His life) in common work and deep communion with His Father in prayer.

The greatest part of my Redemption by Jesus took place in secret — in a life of prayer unknown and unnoticed by anyone except His Mother.

He worked as a carpenter and was content with that title, even though the Angels must have stood in awe at their Creator's humility.

He did not preach or heal for thirty years, though both were needed, because His time had not yet come, and He waited for God's time and Will with patience.

He saw me during those thirty years and interceded with His Father on my behalf. He saw me then as I am now and loved me with an Infinite Love.

His prayers during this time merited untold graces for me, and obtained His Father's Mercy and Compassion for my soul.

He wanted to experience the ordinary, common, everyday life of eating, sleeping, working, and praying—to show me that great sanctity is possible by doing these ordinary things out of Love for the Father.

In the eyes of men, these thirty years of Christ's life were so uneventful that they are called "the Hidden Life," but they were so precious to the Father they form part of the Redemptive plan.

The Way

Jesus knew I would need some definite way to reach the Kingdom, so in the beginning of His public life He gave me eight steps, called "Beatitudes," which would be like a road map on my journey home.

After He gave them to me, He proceeded to show me by His example every stopping place (prayer), every danger point (pride), every perilous turn (the tempter), every oasis (love), every fill-up spot (virtue), every storm (suffering), every desert (doubt and aridity), and every mountain peak where I could view the progress made, enjoy the promise fulfilled, and see the road ahead.

It is these peaks I want to examine in detail for at each of these points I can see all the others like a panoramic view from the heights. Each one takes grace and effort to climb, each has its particular fruit, and yet, it is only the overall view and possession that delights my soul.

When I realize how much I have offended God and how lacking I am in every good thing, I become *Poor in Spirit*.

This realization makes me *meek* in my dealings with others.

My heart is filled with a deep *sense of sorrow* for my sins.

God's Love and Forgiveness are such a reality in my life that I begin to *hunger and thirst for holiness* of life.

In order to be more like my Father, I *imitate His Mercy* by forgiving and forgetting all injuries.

This merciful attitude increases *purity of heart,* removing from my soul all resentment and selfishness.

With this self-control comes *peace of soul* and I am able to give to others what I possess—peace.

It is now that my soul, free of self and human respect, and filled with God, is able to suffer pain and *persecution for His sake* with joy, for now I am a son of God, and the Kingdom of Heaven is mine.

I will examine and see how I am growing in each of these Beatitudes.

THE BEATITUDES

*"Blessed are the Poor in Spirit
for theirs is the Kingdom of Heaven."*

"Poor in Spirit"—what does that mean? If I am to understand anything in the Gospel and how it applies to my daily life, I must look at Christ and then follow Him. There must be a parallel between His life and mine. That was the whole idea behind His rather unpretentious way of life. It was all for me—to teach me, to direct me, to encourage me, and to show me the way to the Father.

I will look at the blueprint for holiness He gave me, see how He lived it, and then follow in His footsteps.

- Jesus was truly poor in spirit for He gave up everything for me, even though He knew there would be times when I would not return His love.

- He was happy when people acknowledged His dignity, and saddened when they did not, but He never sought their esteem or regard.
- He was never attached to His own will but in everything He did the Will of the One who sent Him.
- As God, He did not cling to His independence but depended upon the kindness and love of others to supply His every need.
- He owned the whole world but had no home to call His own.
- He was unpretentious in His dealings with others and desired only one thing: the Glory of the Father and my salvation.
- He was not ambitious for worldly honors and the first place; rather, He came as One who serves and sought the last place.
- He was detached and content to have no one who fully understood Him with the exception of His Mother, who followed Him only at a distance.

I will follow in His footsteps by . . .

- being unselfish and loving those who do not love me. When I am willing to love, even when my soul is not

enriched with a return of that love, I am truly poor
in spirit;

- seeking the perfect accomplishment of God's Will in
  my life, according to the light I have, and being content in the midst of darkness and confusion when at
  times I find His Will difficult to understand;

- preferring the last place, at least in my heart, if God's
  Will and the duties of my state in life give me a position of authority;

- loving everyone and being detached by realizing that
  God takes infinite care of each soul, and they belonged
  to Him long before they belonged to me;

- keeping my soul free from all that is not God, free from
  greed, ambition, pride, and pretension, by never forgetting I am only a pilgrim on my way Home.

It is a strange paradox: when I am Poor in Spirit—detached,
free, unselfish—then all of Heaven is mine. Heaven is in my
soul where the Trinity lives as in a temple, and as I decrease
They increase, and "mine is the Kingdom of Heaven."

*"Blessed are the Meek
for they shall possess the earth."*

Jesus asked me to imitate Him when He said, "Learn of Me, because I am Meek and Humble of Heart, and you shall find rest for your souls" (Mt. 11:29).

Peace of heart is mine when I am meek, and I must look at Jesus to see how meek He was amidst the vexations of daily life in order to understand what it means to be meek.

Jesus showed me how to be Meek ...

- when He forgave those who injured Him—forgave before they asked for forgiveness;
- when He calmly faced the trials of daily life, realizing everything that happened to Him first passed through the Father's hands;
- when He lovingly answered the questions of those who wanted to test Him—by shedding light on both the object of their questions and the motives for asking them;
- when He was compassionate with the faults of His friends and enemies, and never thought about how these weaknesses offended Him, but rather, how they

marred the beauty of their souls and offended the Father;

- ❧ when He strove to win the hearts of the people by patience and forbearance rather than force;

- ❧ when He was humiliated by those who wanted to embarrass Him and showed more concern for their weakness than His own feelings;

- ❧ when He was patient with the faults of His Apostles and corrected them not because those faults irritated Him but because He wanted them to be holy. His motive for correcting was always unselfish and in perfect self-control.

I will follow in His footsteps by . . .

- ❧ trying to acquire the habit of meekness by maintaining peace of heart in the midst of unexpected trials and contradictions and making an effort to see God in all these circumstances;

- ❧ responding to an angry word with a quiet tone of voice;

- ❧ being patient with the seeming lack of tact on the part of my neighbor;

- ❧ accepting the loud, blunt, and forward talk of those who always say the right thing in the wrong way;

- being more concerned with how my neighbor hurts himself when he speaks ill of me, than how much I am hurt;
- uniting my will with God's in everything that concerns me and my neighbor, without bitterness, resentment, or anger, because God loves us and permits everything for our good.

This Beatitude reminds me of the parable of the sower. The Master compared the soul of a just man to rich soil that sometimes bears thirty, sixty, and a hundred-fold fruit (Mt. 13:1-9). When I constantly make an effort to free the soil of my soul of every bitter, resentful, and angry seed, then I am at peace with myself and my neighbor, and I "shall possess the land" (my soul).

*"Blessed are they that mourn
for they shall be comforted."*

The Beatitudes are like eight steps to holiness. As I grow in Poverty of Spirit and Meekness of Heart, I am filled with a great sorrow for all my sins and for having offended such a loving Father. Jesus was without sin—how did He exemplify this Beatitude?

- Jesus wept over Jerusalem because it did not know the time of its visitation.

≈ He was so conscious of the hideousness of sin that on the way of the Cross He asked the holy women not to weep for Him but for those whose malice placed Him in such a position.

≈ He was deeply hurt by the sin of ingratitude when ten lepers were healed and only one gave thanks.

≈ He was saddened by those who would not follow Him because they were so bogged down with possessions.

I will follow in His footsteps by . . .

≈ being truly sorry for ever having offended such a loving God;

≈ occasionally reviewing my life to bring to mind the wonderful Mercy of God in my regard;

≈ realizing that even though I may have loved Him too little, it is never too late;

≈ recognizing my miseries and sins as they really are, and if I cannot weep tears of repentance over them, I will at least accept the trials and sufferings of daily life in reparation for them;

≈ staying away from any occasion that may tempt me to displease the Lord.

To mourn is not only to be repentant over my sins but to be compassionate with others whose sins and faults offend me, and then the Father Himself will comfort me.

"Blessed are they who hunger and thirst
for what is right: they shall be satisfied."

After repentance and an awareness of God's Mercy and Love, the soul yearns for virtue and holiness of life. It realizes the one thing necessary and begins to long for more union with God who is the object of its love.

Jesus is Holiness itself and it is from this Fountain of Life that I must drink if I am to be filled with grace. What does it mean to be holy? What is it that I must desire in order to be satisfied?

Jesus showed me what it means to be holy when ...

- He did His Father's Will no matter how difficult it was to accomplish.
- He acted in the same way as the Father by being merciful to sinners, forgiving those who offended Him, loving those who did not love Him in return, and being compassionate with the faults of others.

- He preferred the Father to all things though He never disdained the things the Father created.
- He accepted with love and serenity the ingratitude of those He healed, the jealousy of those in authority, and the incredulity of His relatives.
- His great miracles became common occurrences when He unselfishly gave His Apostles the same Power He had received from the Father.
- Nothing deterred Him from seeking, seeing, and doing the Father's Will in everything.
- His Love was strong because it was built on sacrifice and not on personal satisfaction.
- He spent much time with the Father in prayer, talking over the day's events and plans for the future.
- He was so absorbed in the Father that He saw every human occurrence in the light of Eternity.
- He gave Himself completely to His neighbor and yet never lost sight of the Father.
- He combined total dedication to God with concern for His neighbor, but was careful that neither one was out of focus.

I will follow in His footsteps by ...

- putting God and the Kingdom in the first place;
- doing God's Will moment to moment as He presents it to me for my acceptance;
- loving my neighbor unselfishly and not trying to make him over into my image;
- spending some time each day in prayer and planning ways of overcoming my faults;
- understanding that my example exerts a more powerful influence over my neighbor than my words;
- being honest in my relationship with God, myself, and my neighbor;
- making sure my desire for holiness and my effort to attain holiness grow proportionately;
- being careful that my goal to become holy with God's grace supersedes every other goal.

To hunger and thirst after holiness is to be a person of unbounded desires. I must understand that my primary role in attaining holiness is to have great desire for high union with God—and He will satisfy them beyond my wildest dreams.

*"Blessed are the Merciful
for they shall obtain Mercy."*

Each Beatitude dovetails into the other and I realize that as I make progress in holiness I become more Merciful toward the sins and imperfections of my neighbor. The whole life of Jesus portrayed the Merciful Love of the Father — to give me hope in His Goodness.

Jesus showed Mercy when . . .

- He gave Judas the opportunity and grace to choose between attaining great holiness or satisfying his own greed;
- He forgot His own feelings and tried to show the Pharisees, lawyers, and doctors of the law, that they must reform in order to enter the Kingdom;
- He offered light and grace to the Samaritan woman before she acknowledged her sins;
- He ate with tax collectors and sinners to give them the opportunity for repentance;
- His Goodness brought forth from sinners a depth of repentant love they never knew existed;
- He healed men's bodies in order to reach their souls;

- He reached out for sinners, for the poor, the sick, the ignorant, and the destitute, with loving compassion;
- He taught with word pictures, called "Parables," like the Prodigal Son, Good Shepherd, Good Samaritan, and the Lost Drachma.

I will follow in His footsteps by ...

- not judging my neighbor's motives and giving him the benefit of the doubt;
- forgiving seventy times seven times because my Father has forgiven me seventy million times seventy million;
- being kind to anyone who offends me and praying for them as I would a dear friend;
- being loving to those who offend me because they have given me the opportunity to be Merciful as my Heavenly Father is Merciful;
- being sympathetic with my neighbor because I realize the depths of my own misery.

It seems to me that the essence of Mercy was expressed by our dear Lord when He said, "He that is without sin, let him cast the first stone" (Jn. 8:7). If I use that truth as a guideline in my dealings with my neighbor, I, too, will obtain Mercy.

"Blessed are the Pure of Heart for they shall see God."

The Master said, "... whatever goes into a man from the outside cannot make him unclean because it does not go into his heart ... it is what comes out of a man that makes him unclean—it is from men's hearts that evil intentions emerge: fornication, theft, murder, adultery, avarice, malice, deceit, indecency, envy, pride, and folly. All these evil things that come from within make a man unclean" (Mk. 7:18-19, 20-23).

When Jesus told me what it meant to be unclean, He was also giving me an example of Purity of Heart. With the above quotation in mind, I will see what it means to be Pure of Heart.

To be Pure of Heart is ...

- to be like a child—full of candor, simplicity, confidence, faith, and love;
- to be detached from myself and not seek my honor, glory, or pleasure in dealing with my neighbor;
- to judge my neighbor with love, and not by the way he affects me;
- to be free from malice, hypocrisy, and affectation;

- to be what I am before God and man without pretension;
- to be single-minded, that is, having one goal in mind: the glory of the Father and the good of my neighbor;
- to take care of the needs of today, completely trusting the past and the future to God;
- to rejoice at the success, talents, and gifts of others, with gratitude to God, the Giver of all good things;
- to be humble in my dealings with others, listening to their opinions, praising their efforts, overlooking their faults, and being Merciful with their sins;
- to be careful that my motive for every action is, first, to please God, and then my neighbor and myself;
- to never lose sight of the fact that my body is the temple of the Holy Spirit and must be kept holy;
- to dress and act in a way befitting a child of God;
- to do my best as I see it in the light of God, and then leave the results and the fruit to Him.

My Father in Heaven, Your Son Jesus did all of these things and much more. Give me the graces and gifts I need from Thy Spirit to follow in His footsteps. I desire to accept Thy Revelations with simplicity, Thy Truth with candor, Thy Son with faith, Thy Love without affectation, the success of others without envy, my own faults without discouragement — and to be confident without presumption, for I want "to see God."

"Blessed are the Peacemakers for they shall be called 'sons of God.'"

Peace follows Purity of Heart when I am in control of my spiritual faculties and I lean upon the Lord for strength, and His Love for protection against myself.

There are many things that happen to me in everyday life that can disturb my peace, but I must make every effort not to let these occurrences enter within my soul and darken it with anxiety, worry, resentment, and hatred. These sentiments are like dark clouds that prevent me from keeping my eyes on Jesus, and peace is nigh impossible.

Peace is not the absence of turmoil, but serenity in the midst of turmoil — a serenity that is the fruit of a deep union with God's Will and love for me, springing forth from the depths of my soul to stabilize my emotions when everything around me is falling apart.

WHAT CAN I DO TO PRESERVE MY PEACE?

After a Fall?

I will use my sins and faults as a means to attain real humility. I must exert every effort to be holy, but if at times my weakness overpowers me and I offend God, then I will use this occasion as a springboard to leap into the ocean of my Father's Merciful Love, looking at His Goodness, praising His Holiness, and glorifying His Mercy. My fall will give me more insight and confidence so that the next time I will not rely on my abilities but on His Mercy and Power.

Humility is the knowledge of what I am and who He is — and Peace is the acceptance of that knowledge.

After I am offended?

Resentment is a long remembered offense and if I am to maintain Peace, my soul must be kept free of the least resentment or bitterness. Jesus told me what to do when my neighbor offends me or returns evil for good. He told me by word and example to pray for my enemies and bless those who curse me.

There is a positive approach to retaining love when my soul cries out for revenge. The Lord is telling me that my neighbor has rendered me a service when he offended me, because he has given me the opportunity to imitate my Father who is forgiving and compassionate.

I must pray for that neighbor because by offending me he has offended God. I must be forgiving and compassionate in order to imitate my Father, whose Mercy is Infinite.

These positive steps may be difficult in the beginning, but as they become a habit I will be able to maintain Peace of soul no matter what offense is given me.

After Ingratitude?
It is so hard to stay close to God after I have tried to do a kind deed, or have given my time, labor, goods, and advice to a neighbor, only to receive ingratitude or insult in return. It all seems so unjust.

I must keep in mind something the Master said to His Apostles. He told them that when they went into a town to spread the Good News and they were not received, they should shake the dust off their feet (Mt. 10:13-14); and again, they were to wish everyone peace, but if it were not received, then their own peace would return to them.

Perhaps this is what I should do in the face of ingratitude —shake the feelings of anger off my soul immediately by being kind, quiet, and praying for the offender. In this way, I do not permit the effects of this unkind incident to enter into my soul and disturb my peace.

If my original intent was to give peace and it was not received, then it returns to me because with love and prayer I have kept my soul in order.

After Fear?

When Jesus appeared to His Apostles after the Resurrection, He often said, "Peace be with you," and "Why are you so agitated, and why are these doubts arising in your hearts?" (Luke 24:36, 38). These consoling words must be imprinted in my soul and brought to mind in times of fear no matter how justified that fear may be.

My Father will not permit anything to happen to me that is not for my good in some way. This realization will help preserve my peace in the midst of fear and confusion.

Peace will become deeper and more permanent as the reflection of Jesus grows brighter and brighter in my soul. It will no longer be dependent upon creatures or things, but upon the abiding Presence of God in my soul. I shall "make peace" by putting all things in their proper place in relation to God, seeing everything in Him and through Him, and then I shall be in truth "a son of God."

"Blessed are those who are persecuted for the cause of Justice — theirs is the Kingdom of Heaven."

When anyone wishes me evil and brings down upon me suffering and misfortune because I am a Christian, Jesus comforts me with the promise that the Kingdom of His Father is mine as a reward.

Why should I be hated for being good and desiring to love everyone? Isn't example worth a thousand words, and yet, that very example is often the cause of my losing friends, relatives, possessions, and even land.

I must remember that good example edifies one hundred people to every one it disturbs, and I must be content with that average.

The person that is disturbed by my Christian way of life has received the message to change his own life, and the Lord may have reached him in a hidden way. In either case, those who ridicule or embarrass me because of my convictions deserve my love and prayers more than any other.

A persecutor renders me a great service by giving me the opportunity ...

- ✎ to grow in humility, strengthen my faith;
- ✎ to unite myself to God's Will, spread the Good News;
- ✎ to portray a gentle and forgiving spirit.

It is no wonder the Master has asked me to rejoice when those who ridicule my faith end up increasing it.

I see in all this a sense of humor in the Lord:

- ✎ People wish me evil and I receive good, by forgiving;
- ✎ they speak ill of me and I grow in His Image by blessing them;
- ✎ they do me harm and God defends my cause; they think I am a fanatic, and God calls me His son;
- ✎ they take away my possessions and home, and God gives me His Kingdom;
- ✎ they inflict pain and I am filled with His joy;
- ✎ they cause turmoil and confusion, and God gives me a peace no man can take away.

Truly I am blessed when I am persecuted for His sake.

Eternal Father, You have given Your Son to me as an example, teacher, and Savior. He first lived and then gave me the way to arrive at the Kingdom loaded with graces, gifts, and virtues. Let Your Holy Spirit guide me in the way of the Beatitudes so that the image of Your Son, which I so dimly reflect, may grow brighter and brighter in my soul.

Amen.

LOVE IS NOT LOVED

LOVE IS NOT LOVED

I am not like a pebble on the beach—a grain of sand on the seashore or just one of millions of human beings past, present, and future. No, I am a unique human being loved by God as if I were an only child—the only fruit of His creative powers.

He loves me.

He created me out of nothing—breathed a soul into my body, endowed me with a personality destined to give Him a unique kind of glory for all eternity because He loves me.

Jesus is the perfect image of the Father. When I look at Jesus, I see the Father—I see Love—I see the Spirit and the Spirit loves me.

If I were to put all the love in the world into one heart it would be merely as a spark in comparison with the love the Heart of Jesus has for me.

I cannot fathom this kind of love because I have never seen a love so great. But is this true? Can I say I have never seen this degree of love? The Eternal Word left His Glory and came down to live among a people indifferent to His love. From the first moment of His entry into this world He felt the coldness in men's hearts and yet, His tiny Heart, beating in the crib—beat out of love. "He came unto His own and His own did not receive Him" (Jn. 1:11).

At the Last Supper, "The disciple Jesus loved was reclining next to Jesus . . . so leaning back on Jesus' breast he said, 'Who is it Lord?'" (Jn. 13:23, 25). John asked Jesus for the name of His betrayer. To deny Jesus the love He deserves and the gratitude His graces demand is a betrayal also on my part. I wonder if His Heart beat faster under the strain of disappointment? Did John hear the Divine Heart skip a beat as the cold betraying heart of Judas turned more and more to hatred? The heart feels and reacts to human emotions and who can fathom the emotions of One who loved with the Heart of God? Who can understand the deep hurt in the Heart of Jesus as the one He loved turned away?

As John leaned upon the breast of Jesus, did his own heart react in fear—fear of the unknown tragedy about to occur? Did Jesus look at John with a heart full of love—full of sorrow in the realization that He could not lift a finger to alleviate the pain in the heart of John as he was about to see His Master suffer so terribly?

The Heart of Jesus—Seat of Love—was torn by love—love for Judas, who rejected His love—love for John, who was soon to endure great sorrow—love for His Apostles, who would not understand His death and so would lose sight of His resurrection—love for His Mother, who would have to stand by, helpless, and see Him treated like a fool—"a worm and no man" (Ps. 22:6).

Mary gave Him birth and now she shares the longing of His broken Heart to suffer for mankind and for me.

I do not understand a love that is fed and set aflame for one as ungrateful as I. My love grows cold when pain and sacrifice make themselves felt. Love seems to be squeezed out of my heart by the weight of the cross. But He is so different. His Heart yearns to prove Itself—yearns to show me the extent of its depth—yearns to manifest its intensity by the lengths it goes to sacrifice.

My love manifests itself when receiving, His by giving. My love diminishes in pain, His has no limits. My love expands when He says "yes" to all my requests—His love was joyful to do the Father's Will even when His request was not granted.

My love vacillates—it is on fire today and cold tomorrow—His love for me is constant and faithful, forever the same. His unlimited and changeless love is like a crown of thorns around His Heart and my sins of ingratitude and lukewarmness are the cruel points on every thorn. When I am hurt by someone, my love grows cold and this coldness hardens my heart. It acts like an anesthetic—it deadens the pain. This is not so with His Heart. His love for me flows from a never ending fountain of love—totally unselfish—burning brightly. It continues to burn for me and because it does not diminish when I offend Him—His Love—His limitless Love causes His Heart a pain unknown to man.

Surely, the Heart that Jesus showed to St. Margaret Mary—the burning Heart surrounded with thorns—was encircled by a combination of its own intensity and my offenses—my selfish demands and preferences. When limitless Love meets selfish pettiness, the force of constrained Love, unrequited, turns around itself in pain. It cannot diminish and yet there is no return of love on the part of the creature so beloved by Jesus. This is truly a crown of thorns around a Heart forever faithful but rejected and put aside for less worthy loves.

Love Is Not Loved

The Heart of Jesus longs for my love because He is so good. He longs to fill me with His own peace—a peace the world and all the things I run after cannot give. He stands at the door of my heart, waiting to be invited in. How often he stands outside in the cold, as He once did in a cave of Bethlehem, waiting for me to acknowledge His presence—to respond to His Love, to tell Him I love Him.

A Prayer to the Sacred Heart of Jesus

Compassionate Heart of Jesus have mercy on me!
The Heart of Jesus is compassionate and understanding. It has felt the sting of ingratitude and when my heart suffers from that same offense, I can turn to Him and He understands my feelings. There is a great difference, however, in our reactions to ingratitude. His loving Heart forgives so easily—mine becomes resentful. How can I obtain that kind of unselfish heart? There is only one way—I need to look at that Heart that is so compassionate towards sinners and make it my own. I must meditate on His love and mercy towards me and then my heart will soften at the next blow—the next pain—it will

not harden itself against suffering. My heart is cold, selfish, and indifferent, but the light radiating from His Heart will touch mine and change it like the sun peeking through the dark clouds.

Gentle Heart of Jesus make me meek and humble.

One day Jesus was talking to His Apostles and He said, "Come to me, all you who labour and are overburdened, and I will give you rest. Shoulder my yoke and learn from Me, for I am gentle and humble in Heart and you will find rest for your souls" (Matt. 11:28-29).

Jesus asks me to go to Him when I am overburdened. He did not promise to take away those burdens, for I must carry mine as He carried His. But I can make them lighter by going to Jesus — by placing them in His Heart. When I do that He promised to make those burdens His own for He asked me to shoulder His yoke. My crosses become His Crosses because His Sacred Heart takes whatever pain I suffer and feels it with me. His love for me reaches into my heart, takes the pain and makes it His own. Love shares not only joy, but suffering. Love feels the agonies of the beloved more keenly for the force of love intensifies every pain and every trial.

Jesus feels my sorrow greater than I for His love is infinite and he suffers in an infinite way. He has done something greater than take away my sufferings—He has made them His very own. He wants me to bear those sufferings in the same way He bore His in His life—meekly and with a humble heart.

He does not want the bitterness of what I may consider undeserved suffering to harden my heart and make it a vessel of resentment.

He does not want the fire of anger to consume and destroy the very tissues of my heart. The injustices He suffered never lessened His love or His desire to do the Father's Will. He kept His eyes on the Father for He placed His burden in the Father's Heart.

He told His Apostles, "No one has ever seen God: it is only the Son who is nearest to the Father's heart who has made Him known" (Jn. 1:18). Jesus, who was so close to the Father's Heart, manifested the perfections of the Father. I can see the Father in Jesus for they are one. So it must be with me. I must stay close to the fire of love in the Heart of Jesus. I must see how that Heart reacted to life's sufferings and then react to those trials with the same love and humility as Jesus.

As Jesus showed the whole world the Father—"He who sees me sees the Father," so I must show the world the loving Heart of Jesus by possessing that Heart as my own (Jn. 14:9). Dare I aspire to that degree of holiness that could say, "He who sees me, sees Jesus?" Yes, I may so desire for that is the "rest" He promised if I learned from His Heart the secrets of peaceful living.

Merciful Heart of Jesus teach me to forgive.
Shortly after they crucified Jesus He said, "Father, forgive them; they do not know what they are doing" (Luke 23:34). Surely, this beautiful mercy shows me the intensity of His Love! He cannot stop loving—He cannot condemn even in the midst of monstrous injustice! He leaves judgment to the Father. His Heart is meek and humble to the last and He seeks clemency on the very ones who caused His agony. The mercy of God was there—ready to forgive the very men who hated Him. The question is whether their hearts ever became repentant in order to receive the mercy offered to them. The Heart of Jesus always extends mercy to me. It is my heart that finds repentance difficult. I need never worry about His merciful Heart—it is my pride and unrepentant heart that can cause me to fail Him and reject Him. In order to keep from falling into

that pit of never ending darkness, I must be always merciful and forgiving. I cannot look at the injustice or offense done to me. Like Jesus I must possess a Heart ever ready to intercede for the very ones who offend me. My heart should radiate the love of Jesus to the extent of never being lessened by injury—never diminishing because of rejection, never changed by coldness. Love was nailed to a tree by hateful men, but It never ceased to be Love. Jesus, the perfect image of the Father, would manifest the Father's love and mercy to the very last. I need never question His mercy but only fear an unrepentant heart that will not accept that mercy.

Pierced Heart of Jesus, hide me within You.
The disciple whom Jesus loved tells us that "One of the soldiers pierced His side with a lance; and immediately there came out blood and water" (Jn. 19:34). Love goes to extremes. Infinite love had to give every last drop of life-giving blood. We know that there is no pain like the pain of a great loss of blood—no thirst so great as the parched lips of one so weakened by a loss of fluids. And yet, St. Mark tells us that Jesus "gave a loud cry and breathed his last" (Mk. 15:37). The Love in the Heart of Jesus felt the pain of every drop of blood He shed for my

redemption. Every pain was voluntarily accepted and endured for love of me. Every drop of blood was shed and cried out, "I love you."

When the soldier pierced His Heart, that last drop was shed and with it—water. It was Divinity giving Itself to humanity—giving birth to a people freed from the tyranny of the Enemy. From the side of Adam came Eve, created without pain in a deep, peaceful sleep. From the pierced side of Jesus came forgiveness—a redeemed people redeemed through the pain and death of their God—redeemed by the love enclosed in a Divine Heart—purchased by sorrow and now forever opened and flowing with a never ending love—a fountain of living water and He did all this for me.

Risen and Glorious Heart of Jesus give me joy.
"Then He spoke to Thomas, 'Put your finger here; look, here are My hands. Give Me your hand; put it into My side. Doubt no longer but believe" (Jn. 20:27). Jesus asks me to "look." He wants me to look at His Hands and pierced Heart. They are proofs of His Love and Mercy. They shout out in one long "I love you." They are to be my source of joy, for joy is mine when I realize how much He loves me. Joy increases and abounds

when His love for me becomes a reality. I was born into this world by the pain of my mother and I was born into eternal life by the pain of my God. Both pains were borne with love — one finite to give me life — one infinite to give me eternity. Is it not a joy to know I was created by Love, born with love, and redeemed through Love? Yes, St. John tells us clearly, "This is the Love I mean: not our love for God, but God's love for us when He sent His Son to be the sacrifice that takes our sins away" (1 Jn. 4:10).

Joy and peace do not come from anything outside of me, but only in the depths of my heart where Jesus and I are alone. It is the joy of His Resurrected Heart that must radiate to my neighbor. It was purchased at a great price, it is a treasure above all treasures — the pearl of great price — I am loved by God — the Heart of Jesus was pierced so the blood of His Divinity and the water of my humanity might flow together and manifest the love of the Father for mankind.

Sacred Heart of Jesus make my heart like unto Thine — meek, humble, and forever loving.
My Jesus, You are Love that is not loved. You are ignored by those You died for and hated by Your Enemies. Your children

have become lukewarm and lost their zeal for Your honor and glory. We think more of ourselves and our crosses than Your sorrow over our sins. As You cry—we laugh, for our minds and hearts have become insensitive to the dangers around us.

We seem to be buried deep in the ice of our indifference, but we cry out to Your sorrowful Heart and beg You to let Your Merciful Love shine upon us and melt the coldness within. We have been deceived by the lure of riches and the spirit of the world. We have become an affluent, technological society, advanced beyond all the ages of the past. But, my Lord, we are still the most deprived, the most poor, and the most hungry people ever to inhabit Your earth. It is sad to realize that in the age when man has spoken to man from the moon, he has not reached or spoken to the God in his heart.

In using the mind You have given us to plumb the secrets of creation—we ignore the God of creation residing in our hearts. We are like children absorbed in building castles in the sand and forgetting the security of living in a house built on rock.

Let us contemplate Your Heart, Lord Jesus, a heart that is loving each one of us with a personal love. We desire to make reparation to Your Sacred Heart by dedicating our lives to following the gospel, to loving as You love, to doing the Father's Will, and to radiating the joy that comes from loving hearts. Our sins are beyond comprehension, our weaknesses like the grains of sand on the shore, but Your love encompasses all things and makes all things new. Let our lives be a witness to the power of Your Sacred Heart as it fills our souls with the fire of its Love. Let all of heaven sing out in a loud voice, "Love is loved by those whose tiny spark has become one flame with the unlimited fire of His Sacred Heart."

MOTHER M. ANGELICA
(1923-2016)

Mother Mary Angelica of the Annunciation was born Rita Antoinette Rizzo on April 20, 1923, in Canton, Ohio. After a difficult childhood, a healing of her recurring stomach ailment led the young Rita on a process of discernment that ended in the Poor Clares of Perpetual Adoration in Cleveland.

Thirteen years later, in 1956, Sister Angelica promised the Lord as she awaited spinal surgery that, if He would permit her to walk again, she would build Him a monastery in the South. In Irondale, Alabama, Mother Angelica's vision took form. Her distinctive approach to teaching the Faith led to parish talks, then pamphlets and books, then radio and television opportunities.

By 1980 the Sisters had converted a garage at the monastery into a rudimentary television studio. EWTN was born. Mother Angelica has been a constant presence on television in the United States and around the world for more than thirty-five years. Innumerable conversions to the Catholic Faith have been attributed to her unique gift for presenting the gospel: joyful but resolute, calming but bracing.

Mother Angelica spent the last years of her life cloistered in the second monastery she founded: Our Lady of the Angels in Hanceville, Alabama, where she and her Nuns dedicated themselves to prayer and adoration of Our Lord in the Most Blessed Sacrament.